The
ART
of
FOOD

Culinary inspirations from
the paintings of the
great masters

CLAIRE
CLIFTON

The ART of FOOD

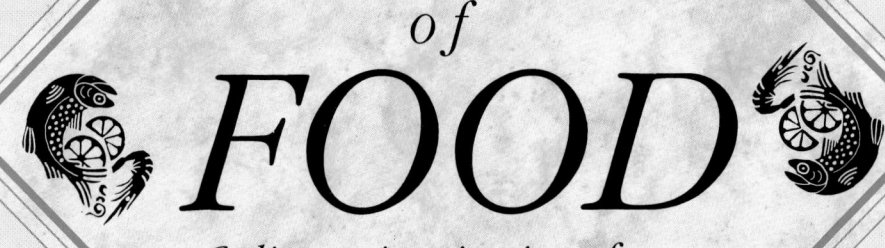

*Culinary inspirations from
the paintings of the
great masters*

— • —

*CLAIRE
CLIFTON*

THE WELLFLEET PRESS
WELLFLEET

A QUARTO BOOK

Published by Wellfleet Press
110 Enterprise Avenue,
Secaucus, New Jersey 07094

ISBN 1 55521 266 2

This book was designed and produced by
Quarto Publishing plc
The Old Brewery
6 Blundell Street
London N7 9BH

SENIOR EDITOR: Denis Kennedy
PROJECT EDITOR: Susan Berry

DESIGNER: Peter Bridgewater
DESIGN STYLIST: Ursula Dawson

PICTURE RESEARCHER: Celestine Dars

ART DIRECTOR: Moira Clinch
EDITORIAL DIRECTOR: Carolyn King

Typeset by CST, Eastbourne
Manufactured in Hong Kong by
Regent Publishing Services Ltd
Printed in Hong Kong by South Sea Int'l Press Ltd.

Frontispiece: Broad Beans by *Giovanna Garzoni*

CONTENTS

INTRODUCTION

BASKET OF FRUIT

Jacques Linard 1600-1645
Musée de Louvre, Paris

As the works of art reproduced in this book demonstrate, the variety of ways in which food has been portrayed by artists throughout the centuries are as diverse as the ingredients themselves. In some paintings, it has been chosen simply for its beauty: Gauguin's still life of luscious mangoes, for example, Raphaelle Peale's watermelon and James Ensor's humble rhubarb. But the rare and exotic food so often a subject of Dutch still lifes in the 17th century appealed to the artists of the time not only because it was wonderful to look at and a challenge to paint, but because it so obviously reflected the taste and wealth of their patrons. In some of these paintings there is a deeper symbolic significance, too, and the lavish arrangements were not quite as straightforward as they seem today. Many contained a message – a *memento mori* (the iconography of which was familiar at the time) – to remind even the rich that life is short.

Food is not only essential to sustain life; it is also an exquisite pleasure. The food we eat, like everything else connected with human behavior – the clothes we wear, the way we speak, the work we do – indicates to others the position we occupy or to which we aspire.

In every society, no matter how simple, there are special foods which also have a ceremonial or religious significance: to celebrate the rites of passage of birth, coming of age, weddings and death. Every community regards certain foods as suitable for different age groups, particular food is prepared for consumption at home, and other food is eaten outside the home. There is special food for illness and convalescence, and there is food that is avoided for religious reasons. There is one kind of food for family and another for guests. There are exotic or rare foods available too for the wealthy and others eaten almost exclusively by the poor. Food that is hard to obtain and therefore expensive is usually considered desirable by those who can afford it and may use it as a way of displaying wealth. A combination of factors such as age, rank and income often determines how innovative and daring people are when it comes to adopting foods that may have been unfamiliar or unknown, or even regarded with suspicion or repulsion by preceding generations.

Most of us in the affluent West today consume food that was either unheard of, unobtainable or disliked by our grandparents, if not our parents. Improved methods of transportation have brought unfamiliar fruit and vegetables from almost every part of the world to even fairly remote areas. A particular item may then fall out of favor once it becomes generally available with those who liked it only because it was hard to obtain, while a universally available food, which is cheap, may suddenly become fashionable. More surprising perhaps is the almost universal acceptance of yogurt, a cheap and easily obtainable ingredient, originally advocated for health reasons, which took root and flourished.

The current popularity of yogurt is just one example of the many developments, changes, puzzles, mysteries and myths that make culinary history so fascinating. It is curious that food, so basic to human existence, has very rarely in the past been the subject of serious academic research. Perhaps it is because it is so ordinary and so familiar that it has been neglected. Only relatively recently have anthropologists, sociologists and historians begun to take notice of food and what it tells us about human behavior. Artists, however, have always represented it, writers have used it as a telling detail to add depth to our understanding of their fictional characters, and diarists have thought it interesting enough to record.

The fabric of culinary history is a richly patterned, densely woven material – as complicated, textured and repetitive as a sumptuous brocade. Cookbooks whet the appetite with recipes but do not tell you the time of day the food was eaten, nor how many people were seated at the table, nor what implements were used, nor seldom what it cost. Other sources are needed. Although there is no shortage of texts, they are often far flung and difficult to find. It is by piecing together the myriad scraps of information contained in household accounts, novels, plays, poems, diaries, cookbooks and works of art and assembling them into a patchwork that the background emerges.

Paintings of food add considerably to our knowledge of what foods were fashionable at different periods and when the different ingredients were available. They reveal how little food has changed. Olives are still harvested in some parts of the world in exactly the same way they are shown being gathered on the Greek vase which is the earliest work of art in this book. But how many of us realize when we eat a humble bar of chocolate that chocolate was, before the discovery of the New World, the exclusive privilege of the Aztec king and his nobles, who drank it out of solid gold cups?

One of the themes I have tried to pursue is to trace the threads that link so many of the dishes we eat today with their ancestors and to tell the complicated story of some of the ingredients. In the text which accompanies each picture I have the opportunity occasionally to dispel some persistent myths about the pedigree of particular foods, such as Marco Polo introducing pasta to Italy after returning from China. Some of them will, no doubt, still be the subject of speculation.

In focusing on the illustrations, I have attempted to illuminate some aspect and also to entertain. Each piece is accompanied by a recipe taken from a book of the period of the painting, wherever possible, chosen not only to give an authentic flavor of the time but, perhaps more important, with a desire to appeal to the modern cook. (The ingredients have been translated into currently used measurements.) Some of the recipes are easier to prepare than others, but the principal aim was to provide pleasure for both the cook who prepares them and those who eat the results. As Molly Keane, who brilliantly described food in her novels, wrote in *Loving without Tears*: "Is there any feeling stronger than that we have for food — nothing more living than the gratitude we feel toward the artist who prepared it?"

Claire Clifton
London 1988

FEAST IN THE HOUSE OF LEVY

Paolo Veronese 1528-1588
National Gallery of Victoria, Melbourne

Proverbes, *Anon, Flemish, 17th century*
Musée de Berry, Bourges

CHAPTER ONE

PLAIN
FARE

The everyday food of people

from all over the world

— from humble peasants to

solid bourgeois families

HARVESTING THE OLIVES

Vase, c. 530 BC

LONDON (BRITISH MUSEUM)

The artist who decorated this vase chose a scene that would have been familiar to anyone in ancient Greece: the olive and the vine were the most important elements in the economy. One olive tree could provide a peasant family with all the olives they could eat, oil for cooking and for their lamps, and for rubbing on the body to protect against cold. When Athens decreed that olives should be grown in preference to wheat it seemed a sensible enough decision – for the olive is hardy and long lived, thrives in poor soil and needs little water. But its deep tap-root eventually caused such severe soil erosion that by the fourth century BC Plato was lamenting that bare white limestone had taken the place of green meadows.

The essential olive was thought to be of divine origin, a gift from Athena, the goddess of wisdom, and oil from the sacred grove of olive trees was used to anoint athletes. Its powerful religious significance endured. According to the Bible the olive was one of the fruits promised to the Jews in Canaan. Olive wood was used in the building of the tabernacle of Solomon's temple and olive oil burned in the sanctuary lamps of Jewish temples and Christian churches, and was used in the coronation rituals of France and England. Olive leaves were found in the crown of justification on the head of Tut-ank-Amon. The olive represented victory to the Greeks and peace and plenty to the Hebrews. The olive branch is still an international symbol of peace.

The poor of ancient Greece lived mainly on *maza*, a barley cake which was made into a porridge, in common with the poor who depend on grains all over the world, even today. A banquet for the more fortunate, on the other hand, was sumptuous. Described by Philoxenus of Cythera (*c.* 436–380 BC), each table was first provided with barley cakes in baskets, then came the course of fish – eels, a stuffed conger, sword fish, cuttle fish and the long hairy "polypus" (octopus). This was followed by honeyed squills, sweet cakes and large wheaten buns and then the meat course – roast loin of pork, boar's head, cutlets of kid, boiled pig's trotters, ribs of beef, lamb, hares and poultry. The meal was rounded off with honey, clotted cream and cheese.

Olive oil, unlike other vegetable oils (which require chemical extraction and heat refining) retains essential vitamins as the fruit is simply pressed to extract the oils. Cold-pressed virgin olive oil (the best there is) is a monosaturate oil, rich in vitamins E, K, F and beta carotenes. Recent research suggests that a diet rich in olive oil results in lower serum cholesterol. The incidence of coronary disease is particularly low in Greece and southern Italy, where it is the most widely used oil.

Olive oil was listed among 700 therapeutics in the Ebers papyrus discovered in Egypt and dating from 1550 BC. It is used medicinally to protect against infection and to soothe wounded or irritated internal or external tissues. Its ability to be easily assimilated enables it to be used to convey medicine that is injected intramuscularly.

Delicatessens owned by Greek Cypriots often sell green olives that have been marinated with garlic and coriander seeds. No cookbooks, as such, have survived from ancient Greece but as so much Greek food is traditional perhaps olives flavored in this way were known to the harvesters on this vase. It is a good method for improving the flavor of olives sold in vacuum bags.

GARLIC AND CORIANDER OLIVES

"Drain one bag of green olives and place in a clean jar. Add the peeled and lightly crushed cloves from one head of garlic and 2 tablespoonsful of coriander seeds crushed a little in a mortar. Fill up the jar with olive oil, making sure that the olives are completely covered. Store in a cool place and leave for at least a week for the flavor to develop."

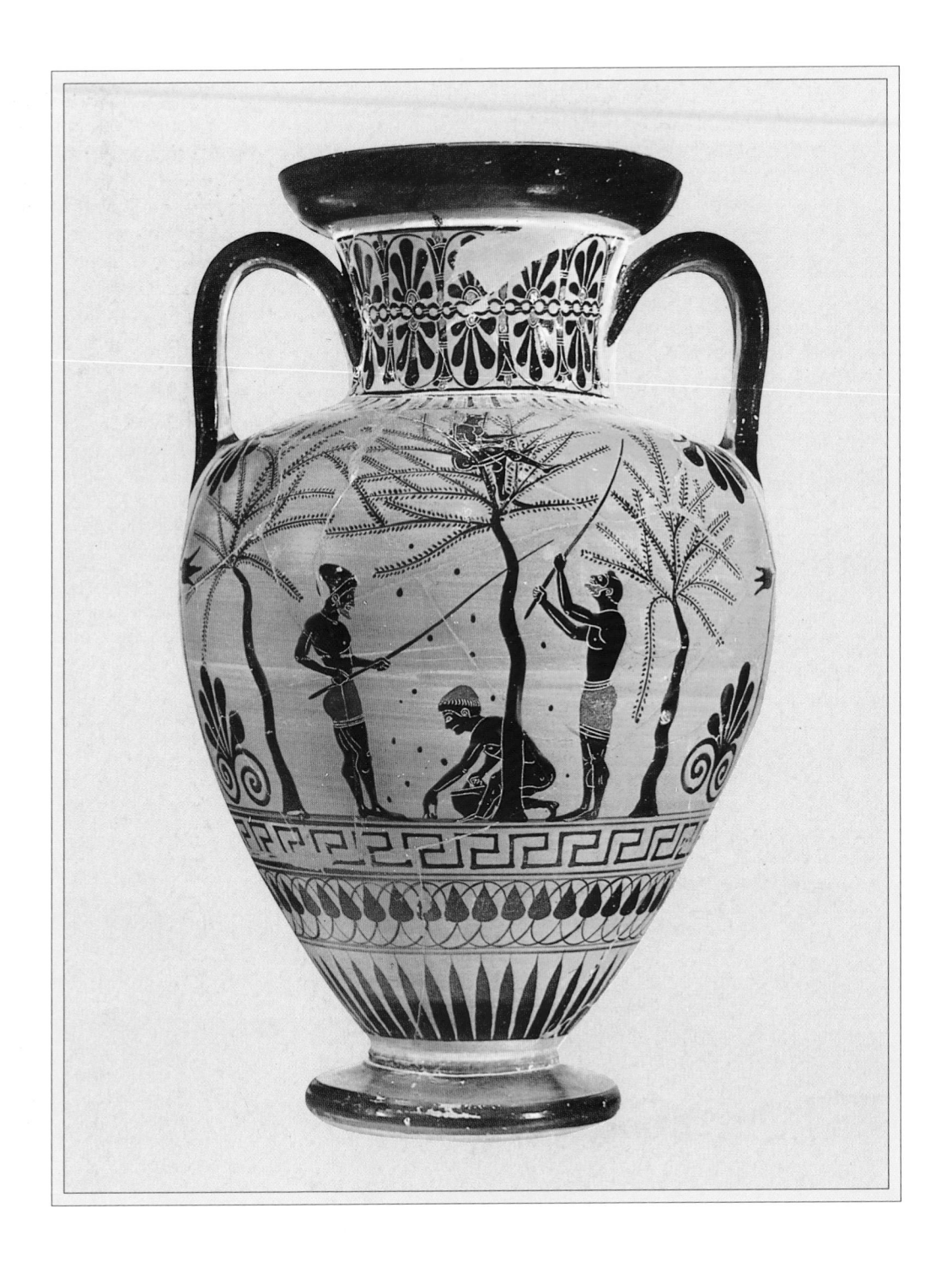

PLATE WITH FISH

Roman, 4th century BC

NAPLES (ARCHAEOLOGICAL MUSEUM)

It is highly likely that this glazed earthenware dish, made in the fourth century BC in Campania in south-west Italy, with its simple decoration of a fish was used to serve cooked fish. The word dish comes from the Latin, *discus*, used to describe all kinds of round plates and dishes used for serving food.

Although the dish here is several hundred years older than the only surviving collection of Roman recipes, it is safe to assume that at least some of them would have been familiar to the artist who painted it and the people who ate off it. Very few recipes are totally new, as you will find if you compare any modern cookery book with, say, the first cookbook written in English, *The Forme of Cury*, compiled by the master chefs of Richard II around 1390 AD.

The sequence of dishes for a formal Roman dinner was very like a 20th-century three-course meal. It began with the *gustatio* which could be egg dishes, cheese, olives and vegetables, raw and cooked: asparagus, cucumbers, pumpkins, herbs, lettuce, mushrooms, salt fish, oysters, mussels, snails or, the most often quoted recipe of Apicius, stuffed dormice. *Mulsum*, wine mixed with honey, was served with the *gustatio*. Next came the *mensae primae* of roast and boiled meat, poultry or more complicated meat dishes. Wine mixed with water was consumed moderately during this course. The heavy drinking began with the last course, the *mensae secundae* of fruit or sweets, or after the meal. Juvenal wrote about a dinner that began with asparagus and eggs, followed by kid and chicken, and ended with fruit.

Among the Roman citizens called Apicius only one was mentioned by several writers as having been the author of cookbooks. M. Gavius Apicius was a celebrated gourmet who lived during the reigns of the emperors Augustus and Tiberius in the early years of the first century AD. The story of his suicide was first told by Seneca. He poisoned himself when he discovered that after squandering a hundred million sesterces on food he only had 10 million left and couldn't face the prospect of lowering his standards.

Red mullet was a fish that was highly esteemed by the Romans. They have even been described as being gripped by red mullet mania in the early years of the empire. They should be cooked with the heads on and the small ones are often left ungutted.

FISH COOKED IN ITS OWN JUICE

"Prepare the fish carefully. Put in a mortar salt and coriander seed; pound. Roll the fish in this, place it in a pan, cover and seal, and cook in the oven. When it is cooked, remove. Sprinkle with very strong vinegar and serve."

Serves 8

2½lb whole fish, cleaned and gutted	2tsp coriander seeds
1tsp coarse salt	¼ cup vinegar

Follow the method, above, for preparing the fish and then bake in a fish brick in a preheated oven, 350°F, for about 30 minutes. Pour some very good quality wine vinegar or Italian balsamic vinegar into a small bowl. With your fingers flick the vinegar *lightly* over the cooked fish just before serving.

THE LUTTRELL PSALTER

English manuscript, c. 1340

LONDON (BRITISH LIBRARY)

The Luttrell Psalter was made for a Lincolnshire knight, Sir Geoffrey Luttrell. The illuminations give us a fascinating picture of daily life in England in the Middle Ages. The people sitting at the table are probably Sir Geoffrey and his family.

The dishes which they are eating must be like those for which recipes are given in the earliest known English manuscript on cookery. A note on the vellum scroll states that it was compiled by the master chefs of Richard II "Kyng of Englond aftir the Conquest" and dates from around 1390. Known as *The Forme of Cury*, it was printed by Samuell Pegge in 1780 and was re-edited and published again by Richard Warner in 1791. The most recent published research on the manuscript has been done by Constance B. Hieatt and Sharon Butler in *Curye on Inglysch*.

Among the recipes is the one here for boiled garlic, entitled *Aquapatys* – an excellent accompaniment for roast meat. Garlic is mentioned in Old English vocabularies of plants from the 10th to the 15th centuries. John Gerard quotes in his herbal of 1597 an earlier writer who said garlic should be boiled until "it hath lost his sharpness." Pungent garlic becomes almost sweet when roasted or boiled.

The word garlic is of Anglo-Saxon origin from *gar* (spear) and *lac* (plant). Garlic leaves are long, narrow and flat like grass or spears. Garlic has powerful antiseptic properties and there are many legends surrounding it. An Islamic one says that when the Devil stepped out from the Garden of Eden after the fall of man, garlic sprang up from the spot where he placed his left foot and onions from where his right foot touched. Garlic and onions are members of the same genus – *Allium*.

AQUAPATYS

"Pill garlec and cast it in a pot with water and oile and seeth it. Do therto safroun, salt and powdour fort and dresse it forth hoot."

BRAISED GARLIC

Serves 4

6oz garlic cloves	*2tsp mixed spice*
2tbsp olive oil	*Salt and pepper*
A pinch of saffron threads	

Put the garlic and oil in a small pan with ⅔ cup water. Bring to a boil and simmer gently for 10 minutes until soft. Add the saffron threads, mixed spice and salt and pepper to taste. Simmer for a few minutes, then serve hot.

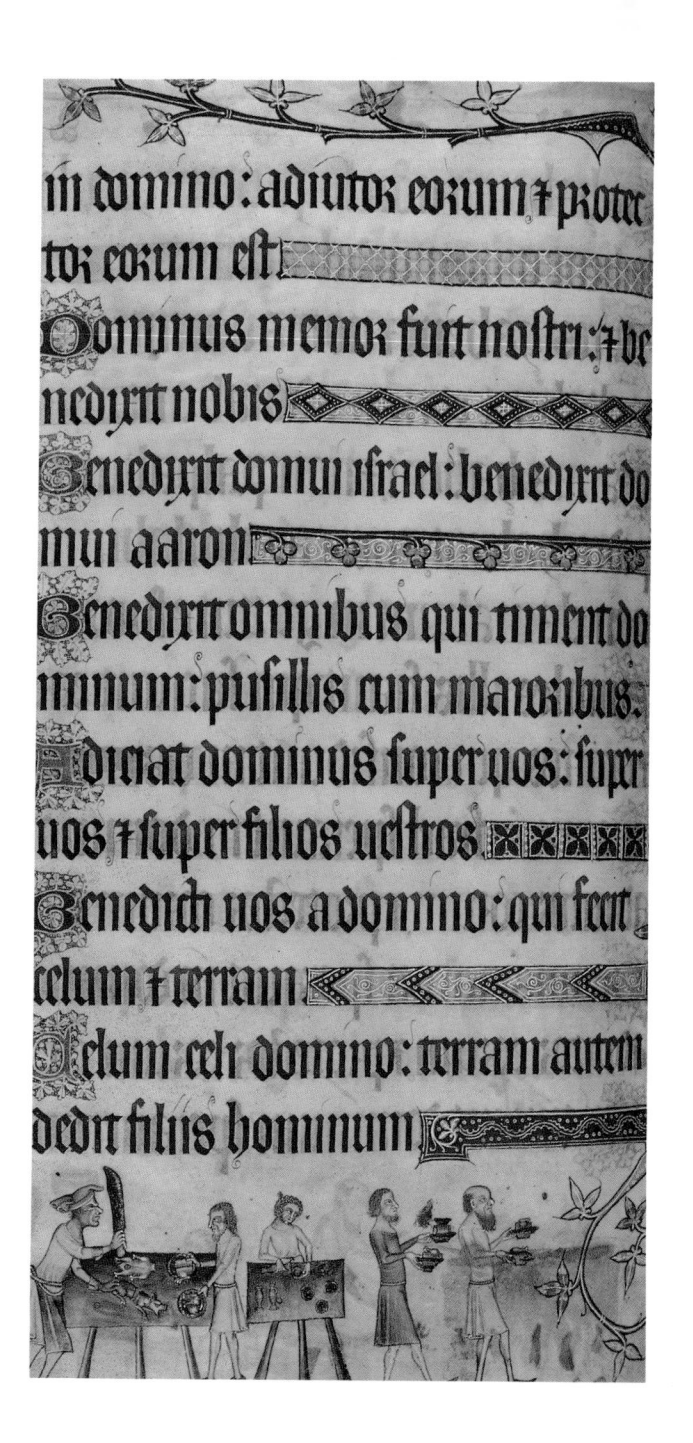

MAKING PASTA

Illumination, c. 1385

VIENNA (NATIONALBIBLIOTHEK)

This illumination of two women making and drying pasta was painted almost a century after Marco Polo returned to Venice after 17 years in the service of Kublai Khan in China. A legend which has persisted for a very long time falsely credits Marco Polo with introducing the noodles he knew in China to Italy when he returned – hence pasta.

At about the same time as this illumination was done, Francisco da Buti was writing his commentary on the poems of Marco Polo's contemporary, Dante Alighieri (1265–1321). Dante wrote about a famous gourmet of his day, Niccolo de Salimbeni who ". . . first found out how to make cloves a costly cult and passion." De Salimbeni was identified by da Buti as one of the 12 Sienese noblemen who formed themselves into the Spendthrift Brigade in 1285 for the purpose of spending their combined fortunes on the most extravagant living possible until their money ran out. They invented "sumptuous and gluttonous dishes" about which their cook wrote a book.

A fragment of that book has survived and is the earliest known medieval cookbook. Known as *A Book of Cookery*, it contains quite a few recipes for 12 people, an unusually large number of rare and exotic ingredients, several dishes which probably came from Arab cookery by way of Sicily, and the first mention of pasta, in the form of ravioli.

Utensils for making pasta, however, were carved on a pre-Roman Etruscan tomb – a water jug, a knife, a rolling pin, a large board with a raised edge for keeping the water in when mixing the flour, a flour bag for dusting the board, a ladle for water, and a pastry wheel.

The Greeks used the word *laganon*, meaning a flat cake of dough which was cut into strips, and the food of the Etruscan-dominated North of Italy was not very different from that of the Greek South. The Roman form of lasagne was called *laganum*, and in southern Italy sheets of lasagne are still sometimes called *lagane* and a rolling pin a *laganatura*.

In the 17th century Italian pasta makers established guilds to protect themselves and by the late 18th century, pasta had become the everyday food it is now. There were 60 pasta shops in Naples in 1700; by 1785 there were 280.

Naples, where the grain ships were unloaded, was the largest producer of pasta until Mussolini decided to make Italy self-sufficient in wheat production. Thousands of acres of durum wheat were planted in central and northern Italy and pasta factories built near most of the large cities. Nowadays, there are said to be more than 600 different pasta shapes available.

There are several recipes for meatless sauces in a Venetian manuscript, *c.* 1385, by an unknown author, that would be suitable for the simple pasta in the picture. They were useful for fast days. One of them in *De l'erbe minute* called for spinach, borage, parsley, beet greens, dill weed "and anything similar" to be blanched, drained and finely chopped, then reheated with almond milk. The author suggests that the sauce below is good with eggs, but it would also be fine on pasta.

SALSA DI FINOCCHIO

"Take the flowers from the fennel and pound in a mortar; put in saffron, nutmeg, cloves, cardamon, yolk of egg and dissolve the saffron. A good sauce during September with eggs."

FENNEL SAUCE

1oz fresh fennel flowers	*A pinch of ground cardamon*
A pinch of saffron strands	*seeds*
A pinch of grated nutmeg	*2 egg yolks*
A pinch of ground cloves	*2–3tbsp olive oil*

Chop the fennel flowers roughly. Soak the saffron in 1tbsp boiling water for 5 minutes. Put the fennel, saffron and its water into a bowl with the spices, and pound together until a smooth paste is formed. Add the egg yolks and oil gradually, pounding together to make a thick sauce.

GLUTTONY

Hieronymus Bosch (c. 1450–1516)

MADRID (PRADO)

It is a tribute to the genius of the Flemish painter, Hieronymus Bosch, that his fantastic images not only puzzled some of his contemporaries but have subsequently provoked scholars to search for the source of his inspiration. One theory is that the bizarre and grotesque elements in his work had their origins in folklore and in medieval mystery plays and pageants. Another suggests that they are connected to his membership of a secret heretical society that employed strange symbols and rituals.

Although his powerful creations did not necessarily appeal to everyone, they were collected by the noble and discerning. Philip II of Spain, a deeply religious man, was an avid collector of Bosch's work, including a painted table top which he installed in his palace, the Escorial, in 1574. (The Prado Museum now houses one of the finest Bosch collections in the world.)

The table top depicts the seven deadly sins: this detail from it illustrates the sin of Gluttony. In it, the unattractive peasant family, with their obese, grasping toddler, are intent on gorging themselves with as much food as possible. The scene represents the bad example the older generation all too often sets for the younger – a recurring theme of Bosch's.

The seven deadly sins and the horrible consequences for sinners in a terrifying hell were constantly thundered from the pulpit, as well as being portrayed in poetry and art. As a result hell was very real to the medieval Christian, but the exquisite delights of paradise – the reward of the good and just – were equally real. Both were prominent features of Bosch's paintings.

Every one of the seven deadly sins was described in pitiless detail by *Le Ménagier* (or the Goodman of Paris) whose book was written in the fourteenth century. He explained them to his bride, as part of her Christian education. Gluttony, he suggested, is divided into two parts. The first is when one takes too abundantly of meat (the gluttons in Bosch's painting are eating nothing but) and the second is ribald and wanton speech. "The Sin of too much eating and drinking pleaseth the Devil," Le Ménagier wrote. He goes on to say that the gospels reveal that God gave the Devil the power to enter into the belly of the swine because of gluttony and they were driven into the sea and were drowned. Just so, he warns, the Devil enters the body of gluttons and "pushes them into the sea of Hell."

He offers a great deal of advice: you must not eat greedily, nor should you chew a dish and choke like Esau in the scriptures. Do not, he admonishes, seek out delicious viands, however costly, and not have enough left over to give to the poor.

A FARCE FOR SAUSAGES

"Take pork, lean as well as fat, and well cooked and hard-boiled eggs. Cut this in dice and pound it in a mortar. Add fine comfits, pepper, saffron, enough herbs and salt in the right measure."

SAUSAGE STUFFING

Makes 1lb

³/₄lb lean pork	¹/₂tsp thyme
¹/₄lb pork fat	1tbsp parsley
1tsp salt	A pinch of saffron strands
Freshly ground pepper	soaked in 1tbsp boiling
1 hard-boiled egg	water
¹/₄tsp sage or marjoram	

Put the meat and fat through a coarse grinder (although a finer one or food processor works just as well), then mix together with the remaining ingredients. Sauté a small spoonful and taste for seasoning, adjust accordingly. This recipe can either be used as a straightforward stuffing, or shaped into forcemeat balls and baked in a moderate oven (350°F) for 10–15 minutes, until cooked.

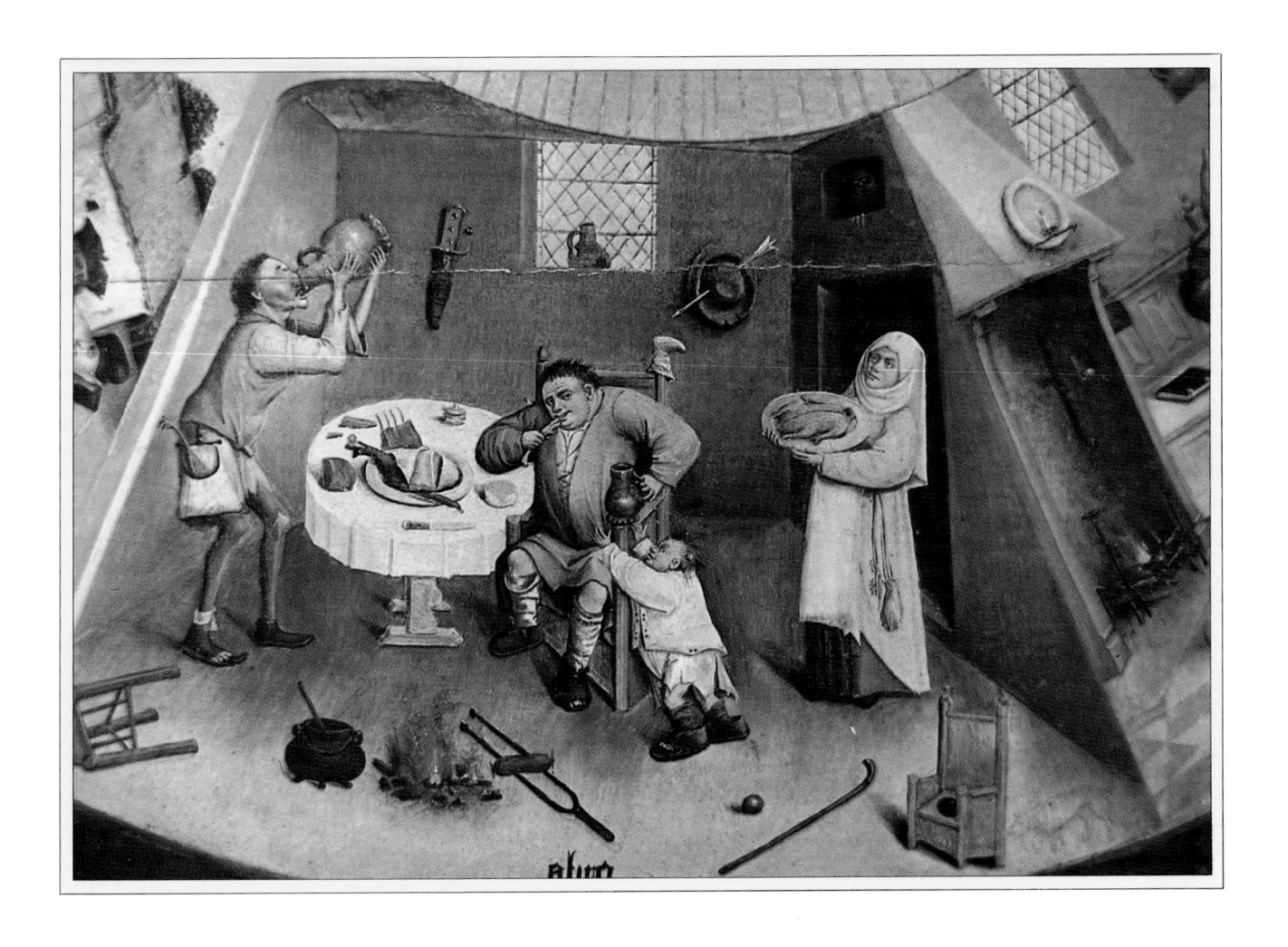

A BAKERY

Franciscan calendar, late 15th century

LYON (MUNICIPAL LIBRARY)

*I*n parts of the world where there is enough fuel to bake it, bread is still the most important item in the diet. "Give us this day our daily bread," says the ancient Christian prayer. The Far East, which relies on rice and noodles, is an exception.

Several words and expressions that have become part of the English language have to do with bread and can be traced back to the Middle Ages. "Curfew," from the old French *quevre feu*, was the signal in the evening for town and village bakers to abide by the rules and cover their hearths to prevent fire breaking out. After the Great Fire of London, in 1666, it was rumored that the King's own baker had not looked after his oven properly.

A "trencher man" was a citizen so greedy and ill-mannered that he ate not only the food that was served on a square piece of bread made from coarse flour, known as a trencher, but the trencher itself.

It has often been stated that the peasantry of Europe demanded, and eventually got, better and better bread. The quality of bread was determined not only by what grains were used but how the grain was treated after being ground. "Manchet," the best, was "bolted" through the finest available cloth. "Chete" bread was also made from wheat, but was more coarsely bolted. By the 18th century silk gauze began to be used for bolting which resulted in fine white bread. At various times in history brown bread has been regarded as something beneficial either to your health or your soul – "Brown bread and the Gospel is good and holy fare" was a Puritan proverb.

The 17th-century English writer, John Evelyn, writing in *Panificium* (a treatise on bread which he produced for his friend John Houghton, who published it) and quoted in *Manchet & Trencher* by Gillian Goodwin declared that in France "by universal consent, the best bread in the world is eaten." His French contemporary Nicolas de Bonnefons wrote *Délices de la Campagne*, published in Paris in 1654, for people living in the country who were not satisfied with the bread from the local communal bake-oven. He gives recipes for all kinds of bread, from wholewheat to white, and states that bread made with other cereals – rye, oats, barley – and faba beans – was only used by the poor.

The ancient Greeks are known to have made bread with olive oil, and this modern version is probably very similar to the bread being baked in the illumination. It comes from *The Classic Cuisine of the Italian Jews* by Edda Servi Machkie, Everest House (New York) 1981.

SCHIACCIATA ALL'OLIO

"*T*hree cups unbleached flour, ½ oz active dry yeast, 1 tsp salt, ¼ cup olive oil, 1 cup warm water, 1½ tsps coarse salt. Combine the flour, dry yeast and salt in a bowl. Gradually add ¼ cup oil and 1 cup warm water, mixing to make a rather stiff dough. Turn onto a floured working surface and knead for 3 or 4 minutes. Shape into a ball, place on an oiled baking sheet and set aside in a warm place, covered with a kitchen towel, to rise for about an hour. Roll down to a rectangle approximately 13 × 15 inches. With your fingers, make depressions or dimples all over the surface. Sprinkle with coarse salt and with 2 or 3 tablespoons of olive oil. Let rest for half-an-hour. Meanwhile heat your oven to 375°F then bake the *schiacciata* for half-an-hour."

OILED BREAD

Generous 3 cups flour	*1tsp salt*
(malted brown or wholewheat)	*¼ cup olive oil*
½oz easy-blend dried yeast	*1 cup hand-hot water*
For glazing	
1tsp coarse salt	*2tbsp olive oil*

Follow the original recipe. Bake at 375°F for about 30 minutes until brown and crisp.

LES TRES RICHES HEURES DU DUC DE BERRY

Pol de Limbourg (fl. 1400–15)

CHANTILLY (MUSEE CONDE)

The Duc de Berry, shown here at his banquet table, commissioned a *Book of Hours* from the Limbourg brothers. It is one of the most ravishing examples of medieval illustration and gives a detailed picture of both courtly and agricultural life in the Middle Ages.

The men assisting at the banquet – the waiters in fact – are wearing swords. They could only do so if of noble birth. The tradition of aristocratic young men doing service in other households continued for centuries. Sir Thomas More waited at table for Cardinal Morton and the son and heir of the Earl of Northumberland served Cardinal Wolsey in England in the 16th century.

An anonymous 60-year-old civil servant who knew something of the Duc de Berry wrote that "Monseigneur de Berry's folk say that on Sundays and great feasts they require 30 oxen, 30 sheep, 160 dozen partridges and coneys in proportion, but I doubt it – Since verified – And certainly tis so on divers great feasts, Sundays and Thursdays, but most commonly on the other days tis 2 oxen and 20 sheep." Elsewhere he writes, "Item, at the court of lords like Monseigneur de Berry when they kill an ox for beef, they make rissoles out of the marrow." This account was contained in a manual of household and religious instruction for the civil servant's 15-year-old bride, probably written between June 1392 and September 1394, the same time that Chaucer was writing *The Canterbury Tales*. It is a lively and appealing picture of life in an *haute bourgeoisie* household. His bride was an orphan of more exalted birth than his own and the week of their marriage she asked him in bed one night not to correct her mistakes before strangers but to tell her in private what she ought to do.

In the manuscript he explains that as he is old and will die before she does she is certain to marry again and it "will reflect the greatest discredit on him in the eyes of her second husband if she is not perfect in manners and morals and fully competent to run a house."

The recipe which follows is taken from Eileen Power's translation of *The Goodman of Paris* (1928).

HARE CIVEY

"First, cleave the breast of the hare, and if it be fresh taken, as one or two days since, wash it not, but set it to toast upon the grill, ie to grill on a good coal fire or on the spit; then have cooked onions and fat in a pot and put your onions in with the fat and your hare by gobbets, and fry them on the fire, moving the pot very often, or fry them in a frying pan. Then toast and burn some bread and soak it in the sewe of the meat with vinegar and wine; and beforehand have brayed ginger, grain (of Paradise), clove, long pepper, nutmegs and cinnamon and vinegar or meat broth, pour it out again and set it aside. Then bray your bread (and not the spices) through the strainer, and put the broth, onions and fat, spices and toasted bread all to cook together, and the hare likewise; and take care that the civey is brown, sharpened with vinegar, tempered with salt and spices."

STEWED HARE

Serves 4

1 hare, jointed	1¼ cups dry red wine
Salt and pepper	1-in fresh ginger
¼ cup butter	root, grated
4 large slices bread, toasted	4 cloves
1¼ cups strong hare or	1 cinnamon stick
beef stock	Grated nutmeg
2 tbsp red wine vinegar	24 pearl onions

Melt the butter in a large pan. Add the hare and brown on all sides. Add the toasted bread, the stock and the other ingredients except for the onions. Cover the pan and cook on a low heat for 1½ hours. Add the onions and cook for a further 30 minutes or until the hare is tender. Season to taste with salt and pepper.

THE HARVESTER'S MEAL

Pieter Bruegel the Younger (c.1564–1638)

(PRIVATE COLLECTION)

The harvesters who are having their meal in this bucolic scene by Pieter Bruegel the Younger, who often copied his more accomplished father's successful subjects, are harvesting the world's single most important food – grain.

Grain transformed neolithic hunters and gatherers into settled farmers and stockbreeders. And when the great glaciers melted at the end of the Ice Age, the resulting warmer climate in the Near East allowed the faster-growing grains to triumph over slower-growing species. It was near the fields of wild wheat and barley that the first clans gathered into larger groups to form villages.

There is still enough wild grain growing in Turkey for a family of six to harvest enough in three weeks to feed themselves throughout the year, as the archaeologist J. R. Harlan discovered in the 1960s. (Wild wheat is about twice as rich in protein as the cultivated variety.)

When people began to sow the wild grain seeds by hand, as they did in areas such as Mallaha in northern Israel around 9000 BC, they became farmers instead of simply gatherers. It took only a thousand years after the first crops were planted in the Nile valley for civilization to advance to the first dynasty in Egypt.

All grains have to be laboriously treated before they can be eaten. The nutritional germ of wheat and barley has to be separated from the bran and the chaff. If the ears of the corn are heated, the outer coating becomes brittle but still has to be removed by hand by means of mortars and rubbing stones. The raw grains then have to be cooked. Originally, this was probably done in a stone-lined pit filled with water. Stones heated in a fire were then put into the pit to heat the water, with more hot stones added until the grain was cooked and digestible. Another method of making the grain edible was to roast it during threshing. It could then be pounded in a mortar and made into a paste by adding water to make the Greek *maza*, the Roman *puls* and the Tibetan *tsampa* which is still eaten today.

If the grain paste is laid on a hot stone it develops a tasty crisp crust – this may have been discovered by accident. Unleavened breads made simply with a mixture of plain flour of oats, wheat, maize or millet and water are still baked. The Chinese have their *pao ping*, the Mexicans their tortillas, the Scots their oatcakes, the Indians their chapatis, the Americans their johnnycake and the Ethiopians their *injera*.

The harvesters in the painting could not read, so they had no use for cookbooks. People at that time who could read and who bought books on cookery were not interested in the food the peasants ate, so we have no peasant recipes except those handed down by tradition. Bread and beer were two of the staples of the peasants and soup made from both is still eaten in northern Europe.

BREAD AND BEER SOUP

"Two thick slices of stale, dark bread (rye or pumpernickel for preference), 1 bottle of strong beer or ale, 1 teaspoon caraway seeds, a pinch of sugar, 1 tablespoon butter, pinch of salt, 4 egg yolks and a little cream for mixing.

Cut the bread into cubes and put into a saucepan. Add the beer, caraway seeds, sugar, butter and salt. Bring to the boil and skim off the foam. Reduce heat, mix the egg yolks with a little cream and stir into the soup, heat through but do not boil."

Serves 2

4 slices stale rye or pumpernickel bread	A pinch of sugar
1½ cups strong beer or ale	1tbsp butter
	Salt and pepper
1tsp caraway seeds	4 egg yolks
	¼ cup light cream

Soak the bread in the beer until soft. Heat gently with the caraway seeds, sugar, butter and seasoning. Stir to mix bread in thoroughly. Remove from the heat. Mix the yolks and cream together and stir in quickly. Serve at once, do not reheat.

PEASANT EATING BEANS

Annibale Carracci (1560–1609)

ROME (GALLERIA COLONNA)

Of the three Carracci cousins who set up an academy of painting in Bologna in 1582, Annibale Carracci, who painted this peasant eating his dish of black-eyed beans, is thought the finest artist. A traveler in the 18th century remarked that his pictures could "vie with the finest productions of Raffaele" and surpassed them all "in beauty of coloring." A guide book published in 1787 advised that "next to Rome the most capital paintings in the world" were in Bologna, "the Carraccis and their scholars having carried this art to the summit of perfection."

The peasant in this painting is eating a dish of a legume called, confusingly, black-eyed beans, black-eyed peas or cowpeas. Italians today call them *fagioli dal'occhio* or *fagioli Toscanelli* – "eye" or "Tuscan" beans.

The black-eyed bean is botanically more of a bean than a pea and is one of the varieties of the species *Vigna*. They were probably originally native to India or Iran but it was from Africa that they passed to Jamaica in 1647, carried by negro slaves. Black-eyed peas, as they are called in America, are an essential component of the "soul" food of the Southern American states. A dish of black-eyed peas cooked with rice and bacon, known as Hopping John, is traditionally eaten on New Year's Day in the deep South to bring good luck for the coming year.

We can assume that the man in the painting is eating locally grown beans. (They may even have arrived in Italy from North Africa during the Roman Empire.) Imported food would have been too expensive for him to buy.

In her magnificently eccentric book, *Honey From a Weed*, Patience Gray describes a method of cooking beans, which is probably how the beans in the painting were cooked. Two special pots are employed, one for the beans, and the other for water to replenish the bean casserole.

LA PIGNATA

"Both pots are brought up to the fire, and the pot with peas, beans or chickpeas slowly comes to the boil and cooks for, say, 20 minutes; then the water is drained away out of doors. It is refilled from the water pot, now boiling, and, with a little salt added and a broken piece of terracotta placed on it as a lid, it goes on cooking. Replenish the water pot – you'll need to refill, as the water is absorbed and evaporates. The home-grown hard little dry peas (they have not been soaked) take about four hours to cook! So do the chickpeas. Broad beans, haricots and black-eyed beans take less. The peas, beans, whatever they are, are strained, but their liquor is kept. A generous amount of olive oil is heated in a pan, some hot peppers (preserved in oil, it's winter) are thrown into it, with a sliced onion, or garlic cloves, and a spoonful of *la salsa secca* (a tomato concentrate of sun-dried tomatoes and olive oil) and then after a few minutes the peas or beans or chickpeas are thrown in, roasting as it were in the oil for a moment, after which is added a little of the liquor and some salt.

BEAN CASSEROLE

Serves 6–8

1lb haricot or black-eyed peas or chickpeas	1 large onion, sliced chopped
½tsp salt	2 garlic cloves, crushed
⅔ cup olive oil	2tbsp tomato paste
¼lb hot peppers	Salt and ground black pepper

Cover the beans in cold water and leave them to soak for 10–12 hours or overnight. Drain the beans, place in a large heavy-bottomed pan and cover with fresh water. Boil vigorously for 10 minutes. Drain the beans and rinse out the pan. Return the beans to the pan and cover with fresh water. Bring to a boil, then reduce the heat. Cover the pan and simmer for 35–45 minutes until the beans are tender, topping up with extra boiling water, if necessary. Drain the beans, reserving the cooking liquid. Put the oil in the pan, add the peppers, onion, garlic and tomato paste and cook for a few minutes until softened. Stir in the beans and cook for a few minutes more, then add the reserved cooking liquid.

THE PEASANTS' MEAL

Louis Le Nain (c. 1593-1648)

PARIS (LOUVRE)

Louis le Nain was one of three painter brothers – Antoine, Louis and Mathieu – from Laon who were all made members of the French Academy when it was founded in 1635. This somber painting of a peasant family is attributed to Louis, although none of the brothers included an initial in their signatures. (The smaller paintings on copper are thought to have been by Antoine and the larger works by Louis.) Both Antoine and Louis painted peasant families. Louis is said to have traveled to Italy, and his dramatic use of light and dark, and the way his subjects coolly stare out of the dim light, suggests to art historians that he may have been associated with the followers of the Italian master painter, Caravaggio.

It is significant that the only identifiable item of food in this unsentimental picture of bleak poverty is bread – the staff of life. Bread, butter and cheese were the basic foods of the poor all over Europe; fresh fish and meat were luxuries they could seldom afford, but dried beans, lentils and herbs, as well as vegetables and fruit (when in season) added variety.

It is difficult for the culinary historian to know exactly what and how peasants ate because cookbooks of the 17th century were aimed only at the well-to-do and did not describe what the vast majority of people ate, who knew by tradition how to cook what they did have. Other sources, though, provide some idea of the diet of ordinary citizens. For example, in 1670 a soldier in the field was allowed 2lb of bread, 1lb of meat or cheese and one bottle of wine or two of beer a day. In all societies the standard of living was measured by the amount of meat and fish consumed.

The peasants in this painting would have suffered from the general shortage of meat in the 17th century and would have been better off in the Middle Ages. Even in big cities, such as Paris, in the 14th century every householder kept poultry, and probably pigs too, judging by the number of laws against keeping them in houses reissued during that century.

We can only guess what this family might have cooked in the earthenware pot lying on the floor, but it is exactly like cooking pots used today in France. It was probably used to cook a stew – on a fire built on the dirt floor of the hovel. They would not have been able to bake their own bread as fuel was too expensive and would have bought it instead from the baker every day. It would have been the main item in their diet and would have tasted like the delicious *pain de campagne* still baked in a wood-fueled oven, and sold at a price no peasant could afford.

This simple soup would have been within the means of le Nain's peasants, with the exception of the capers (although as they grow wild on bushes in the Mediterranean, they could have been picked at home). Country people in that region still gather wild herbs in the spring and summer. The sharp flavor of the gooseberries is typical of recipes that date back to the Middle Ages.

POTAGE D'HERBES SANS BEURRE

"Take a quantity of young herbs, wash them and put them in boiling water with a piece of bread. Season well and simmer. Add some gooseberries for a bitter taste. Add capers if you wish, then serve. To make the soup more sharp, strain out half the herbs when they are half-cooked and to make it greener crush the gooseberries."

HERB SOUP

Serves 4

4oz fresh herbs (such as coarsely chopped parsley, coriander, dill, sorrel and lemon thyme)	2½ cups vegetable stock 1 cup green gooseberries, topped and tailed Salt and pepper
2 thick slices white bread, crusts removed	1tbsp capers

Put the herbs, bread cut in cubes, stock and gooseberries into a pan, cover and simmer gently until tender. Purée or sieve until smooth, season with salt, pepper and capers. Add a little superfine sugar to sweeten, if too sharp.

THE FISH MARKET, PARIS

Fan design, 17th century

PARIS (MUSEE CARNAVALET)

This fan decoration shows the bustling fish market of Les Halles, which was the main Paris market from the 13th century until 1969, when it was moved to Rungis, on the outskirts of the city.

Fish, although relatively expensive except near coasts and rivers, was an important foodstuff in the Christian world. The church calendar was littered with fast days. In the strictest sense this meant abstinence from meat, fowl and all animal products, which included milk, butter, cheese and eggs, but for the less strict, eggs and dairy products and fish were allowed.

Whale, porpoise and dolphin were considered to be fish and the rules were stretched to include beaver's tail, barnacle goose and unborn rabbits. Most of the basic recipes in cookbooks gave fast-day versions with fish stock or almond milk, which was a costly substitute for cow's milk. Almond milk could also be curdled, pressed and drained to stand in for cream cheese.

Wednesdays and Fridays, the days leading up to important feasts, and the entire period of Lent and Advent were fast days all over Europe until after the Reformation.

When Elizabeth of Austria made her ceremonial entry into Paris in 1571 she attended a banquet in the Hôtel de Ville. The menu listed an extraordinary quantity of fish:

"4 large salmon, 10 large turbot, 18 each of brill, mullet and gurnard, 50 crabs, 18 trout, 9 large and 8 smaller pike, 9 fresh shad, 3 creels of large smelts, 2 of oysters in their shells, 1 of oysters removed from their shells, 200 pickled and 200 smoked herrings, 12 lobsters, 24 cuts of salted salmon, 50 pounds of whale, 200 cod tripes, 200 fat young lampreys, 200 fat crayfish, 12 carp a yard long and 50 only a third as large, 18 full grown lampreys, and 1,000 frogs."

According to contemporary reports, the fishmonger who supplied the fish was embarrassed at not being able to provide sturgeon, bream, turtle or even fresh mackerel.

There are dozens of fish and shellfish recipes in La Varenne's cookbook (see page *84*), including carp, salmon, oysters, trout, sale, turtle, and this simple but delicious way of cooking fresh herrings.

HARENGS FRAIS ROTIS

"Cut them and roast them on a grill that is well covered with butter. When they are roasted, you must make a sauce with fresh butter, add a dash of vinegar, salt and pepper and nutmeg. You must add mustard to this."

BROILED HERRING WITH
MUSTARD SAUCE

Serves 4

6tbsp butter	2tbsp Dijon-style mustard
4 × 6oz herring,	Salt and pepper
cleaned and gutted	Grated nutmeg
1tsp white wine vinegar	

Melt a knob of the butter, brush a little over the herring, then broil for about 4 minutes each side. Heat the remaining butter and beat the vinegar and mustard into it. Season to taste with salt, pepper and nutmeg. Serve hot.

THE KITCHEN MAID

Anon, 17th century

LONDON (MATTHIESEN FINE ARTS)

The painter of this kitchen maid, who is glancing over her shoulder at the greedy cat, is known only by the initials "I.F." The prosperous burghers for whom these pictures were painted are sitting at a table in the next room. Joop Witteveen, the Dutch scholar and bibliophile, very kindly supplied the following information.

The most striking element in the painting is the crayfish. It is the only painting known to him in which they appear. Crayfish are not found in Flanders or Holland but did exist in the western part of Germany. As the painting is Flemish in atmosphere, it is likely that the painter was a Fleming who settled in Germany, as many did.

There are several similarities between this picture and one signed and dated 1613 by Jeremias Winghe (Brussels 1578–Frankfurt 1645) in the Historisches Museum, Frankfurt. The rectangular wooden plate containing the fish appears in both paintings and is of a type not found in Netherlandish paintings. Both contain a butchered calf, a chicken, cabbage, drinking vessel and the same three men in the background. The collar of the maid's dress is the same in both pictures. Dutch and Flemish collars of the period were different.

The maid is carrying the lungs of the calf which are the only sort of lungs mentioned in the 500-page poem of the Dutch divinity, Petrus Hondius, which describes his country seat and everything that grew and was eaten there. The poem "Unbought foodstuffs, or the German's entrenchment, that is the sweetness of country life, accompanied with books . . ." was published in Leiden in 1621.

All of the ingredients depicted in the painting could have been included in the *Spaanse Pot*, or Spanish Hotchpotch, described by Hondius.

SPAANSE POT

"**P**ut in a cooking pot all kinds of meat, fowl and game and add to it all kinds of root vegetables, carrots, turnips, cabbage and sausages."

SPANISH HOTCHPOTCH

Serves 6

⅔ cup split peas	1 large onion, chopped
⅓ cup pearl barley	5 cups chicken stock
¼ cup vegetable oil	3lb mixed vegetables (carrots,
2lb mixed stewing lamb or	swede, parsnip), cubed
beef, cubed, and poultry	Salt and pepper
or game joints	
½lb turkey or chicken	
breast, cubed	

Put the split peas and barley in a large bowl and cover with water. Soak for 6–8 hours or overnight, then drain. Heat the oil in a large heavy-bottomed pan, add the onion and fry until soft. Add the meats and fry over a high heat until browned. Stir in the stock, split peas and barley and bring to a boil. Reduce the heat and simmer for 1 hour. Add the vegetables and simmer for 45 minutes. Season to taste.

THE FRIED FOOD SELLER

Pietro Longhi (1702–85)

VENICE (CA'REZZONICO)

*I*t is fortunate for social historians *and* art lovers that Pietro Longhi's ambitious historical painting "The Fall of the Giants" for the Palazzo Sagredo in Venice was not a success. The disappointed artist went to study for a time in Bologna with Giuseppe Maria Crespi and when he returned to Venice he concentrated on painting delightful pictures of Venetian life, portraying all ranks of society, which established his enduring reputation. His work was widely copied by his pupils and other painters and his son Alessandro became a popular portrait painter. Longhi was elected to the Venetian Academy when it was founded in 1756. Although there was at least one important collection of Dutch genre paintings in Venice which Longhi must have known and which no doubt influenced his work, he is uniquely Venetian. Even though the powerful city-state's power was on the wane in the 18th century, the Venice Longhi knew was still a sophisticated artistic center. In 1750 London had six theaters, Paris 10 and Venice 16.

At the time this rather peevish-looking gentleman gesturing toward the fried food seller was painted, the streets of Venice, like those of other large cities, were teeming with cooked food stalls. Their variety has diminished only in this century.

Venice in common with so many other areas of Italy has traditional foods with historical associations. Many of the great Venetian dishes are still redolent of the spices that formed the basis of the overseas trade that made the city so rich and powerful.

The name of one Venetian merchant is still known throughout Europe. Marco Polo was born in 1254 and in 1271 set out on his journey overland to China. He arrived in 1275 and was in the service of the great Kublai Khan for 17 years. He returned by sea to Venice in 1292–95 and died in 1324. Being a merchant he kept a keen eye out for spices. He recorded that Hormuz at the mouth of the Persian Gulf was where the Arab spice ships arrived from India. He sent back reports of spices from places he never reached, such as Ceylon, Tibet and Borneo, and was the first European to describe how ginger was grown and is credited with its rediscovery in Europe.

The Feast of the Redeemer is traditionally celebrated in Venice with *Sarde* or *Sfogi in Saor* (sardines or sole in sauce) – in which the fried fish is covered with vinegar and white wine, cooled, and served with raisins and pine nuts. Many of the sweets that are still made just for "carnavale" (Mardi Gras) and Easter are flavored with spices that would have been familiar to Venetians in medieval times.

This recipe for *crostini* comes from *L'arte della cucina*, written in the 18th century, by Don Felice Libera.

POLPETTE CON CARNE DI VITELLO

"*C*ut thin slices of veal the size of your hand from the leg. Beat them with knife-handles. Make a paste with lard, two cloves of garlic and parsley pounded together, add a handful of grated cheese, together with powdered cinnamon and an egg. Spread a little on each slice. Roll up the slice and tie with string. Put the rolls on a skewer with a leaf of sage between each one.

Moisten with melted fresh butter, some salt and dust with flour and bread crumbs, mixed. Grill and serve hot. When these *polpette* are well made they will bring you honour, in as much as this is an excellent dish."

VEAL ROLLS

Serves 8

2lb veal escalopes	1 egg
(about 8 slices)	16 sage leaves
1tbsp lard or butter	2tbsp butter
2 cloves garlic, crushed	Salt and pepper
2tbsp chopped parsley	1tbsp flour
4tbsp grated Parmesan	2tbsp dried white
A large pinch ground cinnamon	bread crumbs

Using pre-cut escalopes, follow the original method.

LA POLENTA

Pietro Longhi (1702–85)

VENICE (CA'REZZONICO)

The flirtatious cook in this intimate domestic scene by the Venetian painter, Pietro Longhi, is pouring out the golden polenta still particularly associated with Venice and the surrounding region – the Veneto. Maize from the New World arrived in the Rialto shortly after it was discovered, and quickly became popular, especially with the poor.

Maize – Indian corn – came to the Old World with the Spanish and was called, confusingly, "Turkey corn" by the British, Dutch and French; "Egyptian corn" by the Turks; and "Syrian corn" by the Egyptians. It is a member of the grass family and native to North, Central and South America. Columbus noted in Cuba that it was "most tasty, boiled, roasted or ground into flour." It was the most important cereal of both the Aztecs in Mexico and the Inca in Peru. Many of the religious ceremonies of the Aztecs were connected with maize, which had its own god, Cinteotl, and goddess, Chicomecoatl. Prayers were offered to the rain god for water for the maize crop.

Unlike the other New World food, the potato, that became a staple of the poor, maize contains poor-quality protein and is deficient in niacin. In Latin America, maize was never eaten on its own but always with fish, meat, vegetables and tomatoes, and the highly nutritious chilies of the New World. In poor areas of Europe and Africa, maize was eaten mainly on its own. The Portuguese introduced maize into Africa for use on the slave ships. Because maize was easier to grow than the existing grains the first result was an increase in population. However, when pellagra, a disease caused by niacin deficiency, struck those who lived on maize, it became a problem. There was a terrible outbreak of pellagra in the polenta-eating areas of northern Italy in the early 19th century. Although polenta was blamed, the full story of what had caused the disease did not come to light until the 20th century.

In spite of the fact that the reputation of polenta was tarnished in the last century, making it in the traditional way is still a revered ritual – even down to the stirring of it with a special stick made of chestnut or acacia wood. Purists still cook polenta in a special *paiolo* (an unlined copper kettle), hanging low over an open fire.

POLENTA ALLA MILANESE

"Take a casserole and as much milk as you need, and a piece of butter and salt. When it is tepid, sieve in maize flour, little by little, not terribly slowly and off the fire. Cook slowly on a low fire, adding a good piece of butter. When well done and of the right density, add a handful or two of grated parmesan and pour the mix into another buttered casserole. When it is cold tip it out onto the casserole lid and cut in slices as thin as possible.

Replace in a terrine, garnishing each slice with a sprinkle of fresh butter, grated parmesan, cinnamon and slices of truffle cooked in butter. When the terrine is full, cover with more grated cheese and sprinkle with melted butter. Bake in an adequately hot oven till the dish takes a good colour and serve at once."

Serves 2 as a main course or 4 as an appetizer

2½ cups milk	Freshly ground black pepper
1tbsp butter	¾ cup cornmeal
½ tsp salt	4tbsp grated Parmesan
To finish	
1tbsp butter	1 small truffle or
2tbsp Parmesan	2–3 mushrooms, thinly sliced
2 pinches ground cinnamon	

Put the milk and butter into a pan, heat to boiling point, add the salt and pepper and stir in the maize, cook gently for 10 minutes, stirring often and taking care it does not burn. Remove from the heat and add the cheese. Turn into a buttered 8in-diameter dish. Cool completely. Turn out onto a plate and cut into slices. Arrange in an ovenproof dish, with the truffle or mushrooms cooked lightly in the butter. Sprinkle the top with Parmesan and cinnamon. Bake at 400°F for 15–20 minutes or until browned on top.

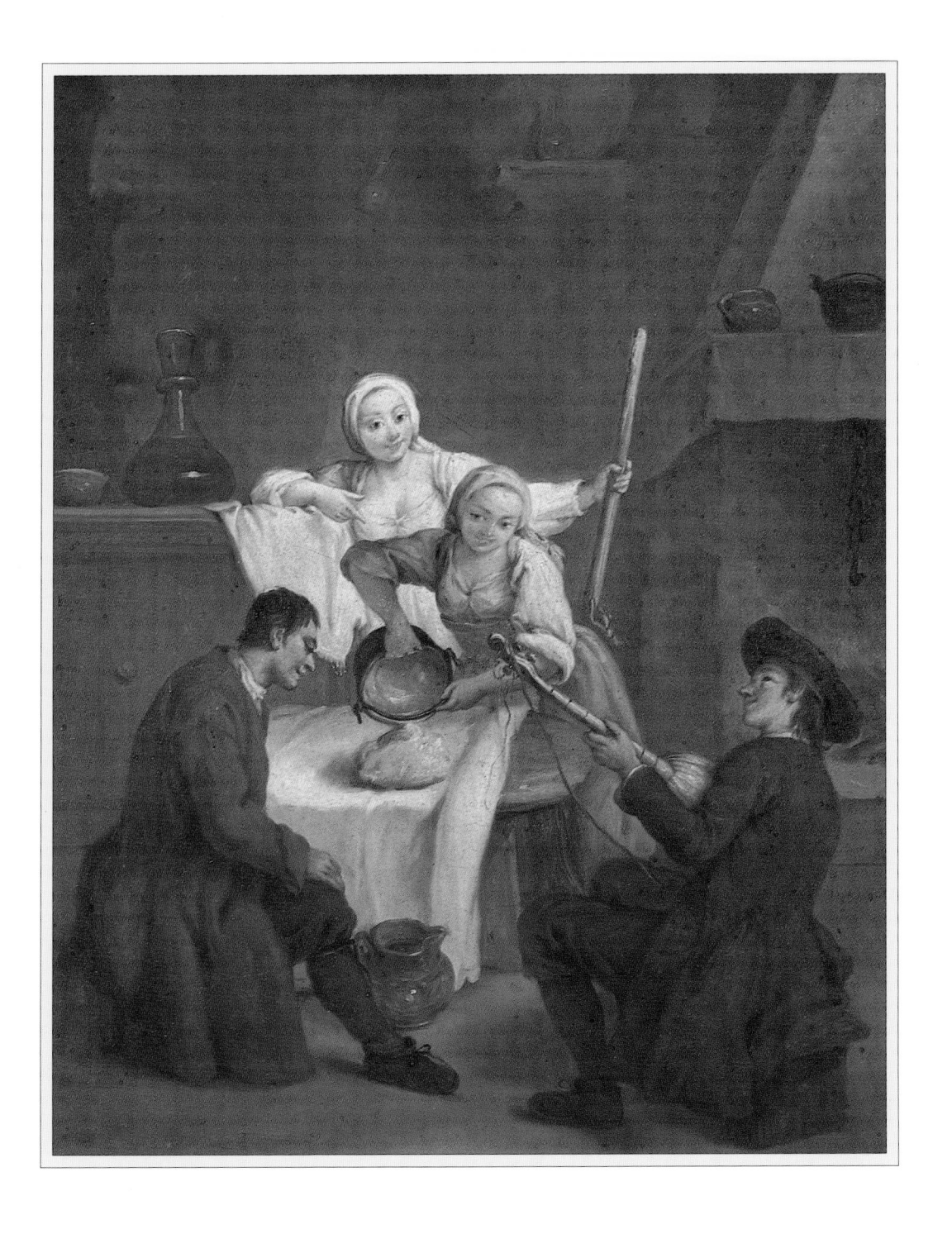

COVENT GARDEN WITH ST. PAUL'S CHURCH

Balthazar Nebot (fl. 1730–1765)

LONDON (GUILDHALL)

St. Paul's Church, Covent Garden, and the tall elegant terrace houses nearby, completed in 1639, the front doors of which opened onto vaulted arcades in the Italian manner, were built by Inigo Jones, the King's Surveyor of Works. Jones had studied in Italy and was strongly influenced by the stately buildings of the Paduan genius, Antonio Palladio. He was commissioned by Francis Russell, who had become the 4th Earl of Bedford in 1627, and to whose family the previously church-owned lands known as Covent Garden had been given after the Dissolution of the Monasteries between 1535–40.

Shortly after the houses in the painting were built the area was one of the most desirable in London but by the middle of the 18th century the prosperous families had left and their town houses were turned into squalid boarding houses. In 1722 there were 22 gambling dens in Covent Garden and the once sedate square was called the "great square of Venus," reputed to be used as a rendezvous by "all the prostitutes in the kingdom."

Covent Garden Market began in 1656 as a few temporary stalls in the garden of Bedford House. In 1670 the Earl of Bedford was granted a licence by Charles II to hold a market every day except Sunday and Christmas Day to sell flowers, fruit, roots and herbs, and to collect tolls from the dealers. In the early 1830s a grand new building to house the traders, designed by Charles Fowler, was erected at a cost of some £70,000. In 1974 the flower and food markets of Covent Garden closed, reopening across the Thames in Battersea at Nine Elms.

In *The Country Housewife and Lady's Directory*, by Richard Bradley, published in two parts, the first in 1727 and the second in 1732, there are three recipes for preserving artichokes; two by boiling and then drying and one by pickling. Bradley introduces the recipe for fried small artichokes by saying "In Holland I have often eaten the small Suckers of Artichokes fry'd which have made an agreeable Dish."

Artichokes may have originally been native to Sicily or Carthage. They were certainly grown by the Saracens in the Middle Ages and by the Moors in the area around Granada in Spain. When Naples and Sicily were under the same rule, artichokes were eaten in Naples and eventually found their way north to Florence. They were cultivated in Tuscany for at least 50 years before Catherine di Medici was born in 1519. Artichokes were considered to be an aphrodiasiac and Catherine was extremely fond of them.

The following recipe is taken from a translation of *La Nuovissima Cucina Economica* (1814) by Vincenzo Agnoletti.

TO FRY SMALL SUCKERS OF ARTICHOKES, OR SMALL ARTICHOKES

"Gather the young Heads of Artichokes, and boil them with Salt and Water till they are tender; these Artichokes should be no bigger than middling Apples; split these in four or six Parts each, flower them well, and fry them crisp in Hogs-lard, and eat them with Butter, Pepper, and a little Verjuice or Orange-Juice.

It is common practice in France, to eat the small Heads of Artichokes raw, with Vinegar, Pepper and Salt; the Method is to pull off the single Leaves, and dip the fleshly part of the Leaves into it and eat that. They are agreeably bitter and create an Appetite."

FRIED ARTICHOKES

Serves 3 to 4 as an appetizer

1lb small artichokes	2tbsp shortening
2tbsp lemon juice or	2tbsp butter, melted
white wine vinegar	1–2tbsp orange juice
1tbsp seasoned flour	Salt and pepper

Put the artichokes in a large pan of water with the lemon juice or vinegar and boil until tender. Cut the artichokes into four or six pieces and toss in the seasoned flour. Heat the shortening in a skillet and fry the artichokes until crisp and golden. Sprinkle with the butter, orange juice and salt and pepper to taste. Serve hot.

THE PROVENÇAL KITCHEN

Antoine Raspail (1738–1811)

ARLES (MUSEE REATTU)

This kitchen interior by Antoine Raspail in the Musée Réattu in Arles in the south of France, looking neither sentimental nor glamorous, is entirely believable. The different social status of the two women in the picture is clearly shown both by what they are wearing and what they are doing. The lady is not wearing an apron, as the cook is, and she is putting the finishing touches to the food while the cook attends to the basic vegetables.

The child, who is no doubt the cook's, is also wearing an apron over its frock. It is impossible to tell whether it is a boy or girl, but the skills the child will learn from its mother will enable it to make a good living. In spite of the fact that a woman would not be hired to head the kitchen of a rich estate, a woman trained as a cook could earn quite a lot more than other women of her class. She also had a degree of independence as her skills were portable and did not require capital.

The author of *La Maison Reglée*, a household manual of 1692, described a full-time cook as "sometimes a man, but often only a woman." A woman cook, he explained, should know "how to make a good soup, cook all kinds of meats, make ragouts with them, as well as fish and eggs, and with all kinds of vegetables for the other days. Also she should not be ignorant of the ways of making some fruit compôtes and a few other bagatelles for the dessert."

If the household was not large enough to include a housekeeper, the cook would also clean the kitchen, dining rooms and stairs and would do the marketing.

One of the most successful French cookbooks of the 18th century, and the first to address itself directly to both the women in this painting, was published in 1746. *La Cuisinière Bourgeoise* was written by Menon who wrote several books on cooking, including *Les Soupers de la Cour*. Both books were published in several editions in France and were translated into English. *La Cuisinière Bourgeoise* was called *The French Family Cook* and appeared in London in 1793. In 1796 it was reprinted under the new title of *The Complete Family Cook* as by that time Britain was at war with France.

Both books are fascinating and full of recipes that could be happily used today. *Epinards en tabatières* (Spinach snuff boxes) are a dainty 18th-century conceit from *Les Soupers de la Cour*.

It is worth noting that spinach recipes of the 18th and early 19th centuries call for blanching and much longer cooking than would suit the modern cook. They are often simply enriched with butter and grated nutmeg or with consommé or meat glaze. Spinach, well washed, can be cooked quickly and chopped finely or puréed in a food processor and the flavoring added last.

EPINARDS EN TABATIERES

"Cut bits of stale bread pretty thick and give them the form of snuff boxes, scoop out the inside without breaking through and leave a border of proper thickness and fry a good brown colour in butter, oil or hogs lard, drain well and fill with well seasoned spinach ragout."

SPINACH SNUFF BOXES

Makes 4

1lb fresh spinach	Four 1½-in thick slices
1tbsp butter	of bread
Salt and pepper	¼ cup butter, oil or dripping
Grated nutmeg	

Wash the spinach thoroughly, cut off the stalks. Cook in boiling salted water, uncovered, for 7-8 minutes. Drain and press well to remove moisture. Return to pan with the butter and seasonings to taste. Cut the bread into small boxes (about 2-in square leaving ½-in border all around and 1-in hole in the center). Melt the butter and fry gently until golden brown or brush all over and place on a cookie sheet and bake for 10–15 minutes until browned and crisp. Serve the spinach in the boxes.

GIRL SHELLING PEAS

W. K. Bigg (1755–1825)

PLYMOUTH (PLYMOUTH ART GALLERY)

Anyone who has ever shelled peas knows how long it will take the pretty young woman in this painting to complete her task. She is neatly dressed, but judging from the state of the wall of her cottage it would seem likely that she is preparing them to take to market rather than for herself.

Peas are a great delicacy, and the younger and fresher the better, as their sugar begins to turn to starch as soon as they are picked. There is nothing to compare with the taste of peas picked and consumed raw on the spot. However, most people in the ancient world probably ate them dried as the Greeks and Romans did. Apicius (see page 14) gives several recipes for peas and named one of them after himself: a dish of dried peas, sausages, tiny pork meatballs, other meats and the usual Roman spices: pepper, lovage, oregano, dill, dried onion and fresh coriander, seasoned with wine and the fish sauce known as "liquamen."

There are, in fact, several hundred varieties of the pea, *Pisum sativum*, also called *P. hortensis*. Thomas Jefferson, the third American president, grew 30 different varieties on his farm at Monticello in Virginia.

The word pea is thought to have come from Sanskrit and the earliest archaeological find of peas was in the "Spirit Caves" on the border of Burma and Thailand; they have been carbon-dated at 9750 BC. This is 2000 years earlier than the peas first eaten in the Near East, in Jarmo in north-western Iraq (in the sixth to seventh millennium BC). Peas were grown in Mycenae. Hot pea soup was the Athenian fast food in the time of Pericles. Stone Age peas have been found in Hungary and Switzerland; Bronze Age sites in northern Greece and France contained peas; and the most ancient British pea was found in an Iron Age site in Glastonbury.

Piselli novelli, the tiny peas developed during the Renaissance in Italy, became the *petits pois* that so obsessed the French aristocracy during the reign of Louis XIV. The Marquise de Maintenon, the King's mistress, wrote to Catherine de Noailles on 10th May, 1695, that, "The subject of peas is being treated at length; impatience to eat them, the pleasure of having eaten them, and the longing to eat them again are the three points about which our princes have been talking for days. There are some ladies who, after having supped with the King, and well supped too, help themselves to peas at home before going to bed at risk of indigestion. It is a fad, a fury."

PEA SOUP

"Take of the best old Pease in Winter, in Summer take green Pease, and boil them down for a Stock, and then pulp them through a Cullender or Strainer with the Liquor; then take Sellery, Endive, Spinach, Sorrel, Charvil, Onions, and Mint, and mince these, but not too small; pass them in brown Butter thicken'd till tender; then put to them your Pulp and Broth, and season them with Pepper, Salt, Cloves, and Mace; put in a Faggot of sweet Herbs and Parsley; stove all well together, and when almost boil'd enough put in a Pint of Cream, or good Milk; let it boil up, and put into your Soup; put it in your Dish, put a French Manchet stov'd up in it, and garnish with scalded Spinach and slic'd Lemon, and serve it away hot."

1lb fresh peas, shelled	½pt single cream
1 stick of celery, chopped	½pt good vegetable
1 small onion, chopped	stock
Bunch of mixed herbs	Seasoning to taste
Sprig of mint	Croûtons and lemon slices,
3½oz butter	to garnish

Soften the onions and celery in the butter, add the peas, the stock and the herbs and cook until the peas are soft. Pass through a sieve or blend lightly, add the cream, reheat but do not boil, season to taste and garnish with croûtons and lemon slices.

AROUND THE LAMP

Carl Larsson (1853–1919)

GÖTEBORG (GÖTEBORG MUSEUM)

Carl Larsson is the best known Swedish painter outside his own country. His work has been well loved by Swedes since the turn of the century and he has relatively recently become something of a cult figure in other parts of Europe. His paintings are admired not only for their immense charm; the tranquil domestic scenes evoke a nostalgia for a seemingly uncomplicated past and the exquisite simplicity of the interiors, so immaculately executed, are an inspiration to contemporary interior designers.

Carl Larsson was born and brought up in Stockholm and studied art at the Academy. He traveled to France and lived for some years in the town of Grez where he met his future wife, herself a painter and a fellow Swede. His wife's father gave the couple an old foundry called Little Hyttnäs at Sundborn in Dalarna, Sweden, which they restored. Larsson painted it over and over again throughout his life. He also made the furniture, carved wood and painted and decorated every available surface – antique furniture, doors, windows and walls. His wife, Karin, filled the house with woven and embroidered wall hangings, carpets, draperies and cushions. The interior, his wife and their seven children, and their intimate domestic life feature again and again in Larsson's work.

Larsson was a prolific artist; he worked in both watercolor and in oils, and, assisted by Italian craftsmen, executed frescoes in the hall of the Swedish National Museum. He is perhaps best known for his watercolors – the perfect medium in which to capture the clear Swedish light and sun-filled rooms of the house at Sundborn.

Like its art, Swedish food is not much known outside the country, although it is both rich and delicious. The potato dish called "Jansson's Temptation" is probably the best known. It consists of layers of matchstick potatoes, sliced onions, butter and anchovies, moistened with cream and baked in a hot oven for an hour or until tender.

Equally popular in Sweden, although less well known elsewhere, is Rose Hip Soup. It is made as follows: a pound of dried rose hips is soaked in 2 quarts of water for 24 hours, brought to a boil and then simmered to a pulp. They are strained, 6 to 8 ounces of sugar are added; the soup is brought to the boil again, thickened with a tablespoon of cornstarch creamed with cold water and simmered for another three minutes. It is served either cold or tepid, with a spoonful of cream in each bowl.

The soup below is also popular in Sweden. Named after the Swedish soprano, Jenny Lind, it comes from *The International Cookery Book*, edited by Ambrose Heath (1953). Simple and homely, it would fit comfortably on Larsson's table in this cosy painting.

JENNY LIND SOUP

"Put three pints of meat stock, or water in which meat extract has been dissolved, into a saucepan and bring to the boil. When boiling, sprinkle in two tablespoons of small sago and continue boiling until the sago is transparent and cooked. Season the soup with pepper and salt, mix an egg with a cup of top milk in a bowl, and pour the soup into this, stirring constantly. Serve at once, without boiling again."

Serves 6

3¾ cups stock	1 small egg
1 tbsp sago	¼ cup half-and-half or
Salt and pepper	light cream

Good home-made stock must be used for this soup. Put the stock into a pan, bring to a boil and add the sago, cover and cook for 12–15 minutes until transparent. Season to taste. Remove from the heat and allow to cool slightly.

Beat the egg and milk or cream together. Transfer the soup to a tureen and stir in the egg mixture. Serve at once.

THE SAFFRON CAKE

Stanhope Forbes (1857–1947)

(PRIVATE COLLECTION)

The forerunner of the Saffron Cake in this painting was a bread or dough cake not as sweet as the modern cake but very aromatic. Saffron threads were steeped in warm water and used to mix the yeast and flour which turned it the highly prized rich golden color. Cream or butter could be added to help preserve the scent and a little honey or sugar to help the yeast ferment.

Saffron comes from the stamens of *Crocus sativus*, a member of the iris family, and they have to be laboriously picked from each tiny flower by hand and then spread on trays to dry. It is the most expensive spice in the world – at times it has been worth more than its weight in gold and has been cultivated since before the second millennium BC. Murals at Knossos on Crete show saffron gatherers at work.

Homer wrote that Zeus slept on a bed of saffron, lotus and hyacinth flowers. It grew wild in Canaan and is one of the many foods mentioned in the Song of Songs. The vivid yellow dye made from saffron was the color of royalty in ancient Greece (until it became identified with the cultivated prostitutes, the *hetaerae*). The Buddhists in India adopted it as the sacred color after the death of the Buddha.

The herbalist John Gerard wrote in his *Herbal* in 1597 that "Common or best Knowne Saffron groweth plentifully in Cambridge-shire, Saffron-Waldon and other places there about, as corne in the fields . . . moderate use . . . is good for the head, and maketh the sences more quicke and lively, shaketh off heavy and drosie sleep, and maketh a man merry." Sir Francis Drake agreed: "What made the English people sprightly was the liberal use of saffron in their broths and sweetmeats."

Saffron was certainly valued for its color as well as for its restorative properties as Dorothy Hartley remarked in *Food in England*. She quotes a recipe of 1700 for "Spirit of Saffron for the Consumptive Cough" which calls for "ordinary spirit of wine, four drams of the best saffron, half a pound of white sugar candy beaten small. Set it in the sun and shake it twice a day till the candy is dissolved and the spirit a deep orange color."

Most saffron today comes from Spain and the best is sold as threads. The powdered variety is too easily adulterated with cheaper substances.

MRS BEETON'S SAFFRON CAKE

"Small ½oz yeast, ½pt warm water, 1lb plain flour, ½tsp salt, 6–8oz margarine, 4oz sugar, 2 eggs, a good pinch of saffron (infuse the saffron with ⅛pt of the warm water, 4–6oz currants and raisins. Cream the yeast and add the warm water to it. Stir into it enough sifted flour to make a nice soft dough. Knead it well and leave to rise in a warm place. When well risen, take the remaining flour and salt, and rub the fat into it; add the sugar, eggs and fermented dough, together with the strained saffron liquour. Knead this well and work in the currants and stoned raisins. Put the dough into two greased ½lb cake-tins and leave to rise well. Bake in a fairly hot to moderate oven (350°F) for 1–1½hr."

SAFFRON LOAF

Makes 1 large loaf

A large pinch of saffron strands	½ tsp salt
1tbsp boiling water	¾ cup butter
½oz active dried yeast	Heaped ½ cup sugar
1¼ cups hand-hot water	2 eggs
4 cups all-purpose flour	1 cup currants or raisins

Soak the saffron in the boiling water overnight.

The next day, soak the yeast in ⅔ cup of the water, leave for 10 minutes or until frothy. Cut the butter into the flour and add the remaining ingredients. Finally add the soaked saffron and yeast mixtures and the remaining ⅔ cup hot water. Beat together until smooth. Pour into a well greased and lined 2lb bread pan. Cover and leave to rise until doubled in size. Bake at 325°F for 1½ hours. Turn out to cool.

MAKING SAUSAGES

Alan Stones (1947–)

(PRIVATE COLLECTION)

Every year the British consume some six billion sausages like the ones in this painting – more than 225 tons – making an average of 125 per head. Every national cuisine has its own kinds of sausage. It seems to have occurred to every group of people which eats meat that the parts of it that are not suitable for much else can be made into a delicacy by grinding it and adding flavorings. By law, the British pork sausage must contain at least 65 per cent meat; beef, or pork and beef, or other meat sausages must contain not less than 50 per cent meat, half of it lean, in each case.

Sausages have been popular since ancient times. A royal banquet menu in India at the end of the first millennium AD included them; there are numerous recipes for sausages in the Roman cookbook of Apicius; and Pope Pius V served stewed pigeons with mortadella sausage and whole onions at a banquet given in 1570.

The highly spiced Lucanian sausages of Apicius, which contained pounded pepper, cumin, savory, rue, parsley, mixed herbs, laurel berries, liquamen, well-beaten meat, ground spices, pepper corns, plenty of fat and pine kernels, were smoked; they may have been at least one of the varieties the Romans brought with them to Britain.

The earliest English sausage recipes, which date from the 14th century, contained sage – still a frequent flavoring. Black puddings were originally made from blood, when the pig was killed in late autumn, and spiced with ginger, cloves and pepper. They were a favorite food for both high days and Holy days.

The white puddings of Elizabethan times were made from grated bread, currants, egg yolks, nutmeg, cinnamon, sugar, salt and beef suet, served with cream; the suet was omitted for Lent. A cookbook from the middle of the 17th century gives directions for a dish of boiled sausages to be served with a sauce of currants. Another recipe of the same period is for sausages, usually of mutton, with oysters (which turned up in recipe books until the 18th century). Mussel sausages were also included in Apicius and sea-food sausages have been revived by chefs recently.

British sausagemakers have only recently been persuaded that sausages need not be vividly colored, now that artificial food colorings have been proven to be a health hazard. The taste for red, or at least pink, sausages goes back to the 17th century when Bologna or "Polony" sausages were made red with red sage, salt-peter and red wine, or cochineal in sack.

Very few people these days are inclined to make their own sausages but these traditional vegetarian Welsh "sausages" are a delicious alternative. Theodora Fitzgibbon writes in *A Taste of Wales* (Dent, 1971) that they were originally made from Glamorgan cheese, made in turn from the milk of the white Gwent cattle.

GLAMORGAN SAUSAGES

"6oz grated hard cheese, 10oz fresh breadcrumbs, 1 tsp dry mustard, 1 tsp thyme, 1 tbsp chopped parsley, 1 small onion, grated, salt and pepper, 2 eggs, separated, flour and crisp breadcrumbs for coating, oil for frying. Mix the cheese, breadcrumbs, mustard, herbs, onion and salt and pepper together. Add the beaten egg yolks. Beat the egg whites until not quite stiff. *Shape the mixture into small sausages, roll in the egg white and then in the breadcrumbs. Fry in hot oil or fat."

*Sprinkle flour on your hands and a working surface.

Makes 8

6oz sharp cheddar, grated	Salt and pepper
5 cups fresh bread crumbs	2 eggs, separated
1tsp dry English mustard	Flour for dusting
1tsp dried thyme	1/4 cup dried bread crumbs
1tbsp chopped parsley	Oil for shallow frying
1 small onion, grated	

Mix the cheese, bread crumbs, mustard, herbs, onion and seasoning together. Add the yolks and one egg white to the mixture. Mix well and, with floured hands shape into eight sausage shapes. Roll in remaining egg white and then in bread crumbs. Fry until golden brown all over, remove, keep warm in the oven until served.

The Five Senses *by Sébastien Stoskopff, 1633*
Musée Notre Dame, Strasbourg.

CHAPTER TWO

COURTLY
FOOD

The rich and sumptuous
displays of high living — elaborate
dishes, magnificent banquets,
exotic ingredients

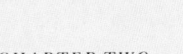

STILL LIFE WITH CAKES AND PARROT
Flegel (1563–1638)
MUNICH (ALTE PINAKOTHEK)

The beautiful pomegranate is a fruit of great antiquity which reveals its "heart within, blood-tinctured, of a veined humanity," wrote Robert Browning. Pomegranates have been found in a Bronze Age tomb in Jericho, and were grown in ancient Egypt before the time of Moses. King Solomon had a grove of them: in the "Song of Songs" he compares the temples of his beloved to them. To the ancient Greeks, the pomegranate, said to be created by Zeus, represented fertility and was the emblem of Persephone, the goddess of spring.

Pomegranates are still immensely popular in the Middle East. The prophet Mohammed recommended eating them to "purge the system of envy and hatred." A delicious concentrated juice is used in cooking, and a sweetened cordial, grenadine, is diluted with water for a refreshing drink.

The Romans imported pomegranates from Carthage and it was from the East that they migrated to Europe. The Saracens reintroduced the fruit after the fall of the Roman Empire, first in Sicily and then in southern Spain where Ibn-al-Awam wrote in the 13th century that 10 varieties were grown. It is now the emblem of the city of Granada. A favorite motif for artists since ancient times, the pomegranate inspired the elaborate patterns, still used today, which originated in the East but reached the height of their popularity in the embroidered brocades and damasks of the Italian renaissance.

Le Ménagier (The Goodman of Paris – see page 20) gives several recipes for pomegranates and they also appear in *The Forme of Cury* (see page 16). They were cultivated in Britain as early as 1548 and there are reports of them being grown in tubs in Wimbledon in 1649. They were certainly familiar to Shakespeare: he has Juliet say to Romeo, "Nightly she sings on yon pomegranate tree; Believe me, love, it was the nightingale."

The dried seeds of the wild Himalayan pomegranate *daru* are used for the Indian condiment *anar dana*. In India, fresh pomegranates, grapes and jujubes (a small native fruit sometimes compared to the date) began King Srenika's banquet, the menu of which has survived from the first millennium AD.

The beady-eyed parrot in the painting, also an import from a hotter climate, may have spotted the roast figs among this decorative grouping of flowers and food. They were described in a manuscript dating from the mid-16th century, discovered in the Dominican monastery of St Paul in Leipzig. Said to be a special favorite of one Bishop John, who heard of them from a monk on his return from the Holy Lands where "the Arabs and infidels eat them on fast days – but there is no reason for a pious Christian soul to take fright at them," they were roasted with sweet wine and raisins and thickened with rice flour.

MOSTACCIOLI

"Take a pound of almonds, peeled and pulver-, ized, 1½ pounds of flour, 4 ounces of cinnamon, ½ an ounce of nutmeg, a pinche of powdered cloves, musk 10 grains, 2 pounds of sifted white sugar, 6 egg yolks, two ounces of butter. Make a batter of it with some rosewater. The batter should be rather stiff. Put the mostacciolis in moulds, small or big as you like, and place them on wafer or paper and bake them in a moderate oven."

ALMOND COOKIES

Makes 24 cookies

2 cups almonds, ground	4 cups sifted
2½ cups all-purpose flour	confectioners' sugar
2tsp ground cinnamon	3 large egg yolks
½tsp ground nutmeg	2tbsp softened butter
A pinch of ground cloves	1¼ cups rosewater

Put the dry ingredients in a bowl and form a well in the center. Put the yolks and liquid in the well, and mix the ingredients together into a stiff batter. Spoon into paper cup cases and bake at 350°F for about 25 minutes or until puffed up. Do not overcook or they will lose their shape. Remove from the oven and cool.

BARON COBHAM AND HIS FAMILY

Anon, English, 16th century

(PRIVATE COLLECTION)

The high position in society of Baron Cobham and his richly dressed family, sitting demurely around the table in this painting, is displayed by their clothes and jewels. The food, though, is far from extravagant, a common feature of the period. The first printed English cookbook, *A Proper Newe Booke of Cookerye*, had appeared 22 years earlier. English food of this century has been described as being relentlessly domestic and indeed the recipes in the *Newe Booke* are mostly simplified versions of medieval hashes and gruels with somewhat fewer spices.

The fruit on Lord Cobham's table was probably from his own estate. Thomas Tusser had already advised in *A Hundred Good Pointes of Husbandrie* in 1557 that nothing should be purchased outside a small estate except capers, lemons, olives, oranges, rice and samphire.

But there were several new fruits and vegetables in 16th-century Britain, which Lord Cobham and his family would have been able to afford. Lemons were mentioned only twice in the Oxford English Dictionary prior to 1500, but they soon became fashionable, as did anything rare and precious. Oranges were grown in European hothouses, and the cucumber arrived in 1573. The new vegetables were kidney beans, red and white beets, shallots, carrots, chickpeas, lentils, lettuce, chicory and orach. Spinach was first grown around 1568 – rich families were told to keep a silver saucepan for cooking it. Parsley was new in 1548 and peaches, said to have been brought back by the Crusaders and mentioned by Chaucer, were probably not cultivated in England until 1562.

The exotic parrot on the table was no doubt a prized family pet but other birds were perceived as valuable food. The four-and-twenty blackbirds in the nursery rhyme pie were a feature of banquets of this period.

Giovanni de Rosselli, whose *Epulario (The Italian Banquet)* was originally published in 1516 and printed in London in 1598, gives such a recipe: "To make Pies that Birds may be alive in them and flie out when it is cut up."

This recipe comes from *The Good Housewife's Jewell* by Thomas Dawson, 1596 (quoted in Mrs Goundes-Peace's *Old Cookery Notebook*, edited by Robin Howe, 1971).

TO MAKE STEWED STEAKES

"Take a peece of Mutton, and cutte it in pieces, and wash it very cleane, and put it in a faire potte with Ale, or with halfe Wine, then make it boyle, and skumme it cleyne, and put into your pot a faggot of Rosemary and Time, then some parsely picked fine, and some onyons cut round, and let them all boyle together, then take prunes, and raisons, dates and currans, and let it boyle altogether, and season it with Sinamon and Ginger, Nutmeggs, two or three Cloues (cloves), and Salt, and so serve it on soppes (bread soaked in wine or gravy) and garnish it with fruite."

Serves 4

4 lamb leg steaks	1 sprig fresh thyme
(approx 1½lb)	1 small bunch fresh parsley
1 large onion, chopped	½tsp ground allspice
2tbsp oil	8oz stoned prunes
1pt traditional ale	4oz raisins
1 sprig fresh rosemary	Salt and pepper

Heat the oil in a large pan and brown the steaks on both sides. Add the onion and cook to soften. Cover with the ale, add the prunes and raisins, herbs and spices and simmer gently for 1½–2 hours until the lamb is tender. Season to taste with salt and pepper. Serve with thickly cut fresh bread and garnish with slices of orange or lemon.

STILL LIFE WITH PATE EN CROUTE

Sébastien Stoskopff (1596–1657)

LONDON (MATTHIESEN FINE ARTS)

This modest *pâté en croûte* is the successor to the "grete pie" of medieval European cooking. The magnificent game pies of the Middle Ages remained popular for several centuries. They were made with pigeons, doves, quails, rails, bustards, peacocks, cranes, swans, moor- and water-fowl and rooks. The quantities of spices were doubled if the pies were to be eaten cold.

In the ninth century, Charlemagne directed his officers to reserve the best flour for making a *pâté en croûte*. The pie had the advantage of keeping food relatively hotter when it had to be carried a long distance from the kitchen to the table. But they were also served cold and, being easily portable, out-of-doors or when traveling.

A 14th-century Italian cookery book gives a complicated recipe for a *torta*, which was the star of every banquet. Layers of chicken fried in oil, ham made into ravioli and sausage are covered with pastry and alternating layers of dates and almonds and more pastry. The same volume gives directions for a pie with live song birds which were meant to appear through windows in the "roof," which was hung on a "tree" of pastry.

In the 15th century, on Ember Days, the three days of fasting which occurred four times a year (after the first Sunday in Lent, Whitsun, Holy Rood Day – 14 September – and St. Lucy's Day – 13 December), a special tart was made, known as an English Tart. It was made with onions, sage, parsley, cream cheese, eggs, butter, sugar, raisins, cinnamon and ginger, with a pastry crust.

The famous 18th-century Yorkshire Christmas Pie contained a boned turkey, goose, fowl, partridge and a pigeon fitted inside each other with a crust constructed to look like a whole turkey. Pieces of hare and whole woodcocks were arranged around the sides and the whole edifice covered with 4lb of butter and a thick lid. They were often sent to London as gifts and had to be sturdily made. There was also a Yorkshire Goose Pie.

Pies are still a feature of every national cuisine in Europe and many traditional recipes have combinations of meat, fruit, spices and sharpening agents, such as citrus juice or vinegar, which date back to Roman times.

The recipe below is a 17th-century one for rabbit pie, published in La Varenne's *Le Cuisinier François*.

PIE OF YOUNG RABBITS

"This pie is made in the same way as a game pie. Lard the cleaned rabbits with thick lard and season them with salt, pepper, vinegar and powdered cloves. If the pie is for keeping, make the dough from rye flour without butter, salt and pepper. Put aside a part of the dough to form the lid of the pie. Shape the dough to a pie and fill it with the rabbits. Shape the rest of the dough to a pie lid and make a small hole in it so the steam can escape during the baking. Cover the pie with the lid and cook it for three and a half hours. When the pie is done, close the opening in the lid with a little piece of dough."

RABBIT PIE

Serves 6

2 young rabbits, skinned and cleaned	A pinch of ground cloves
1oz larding fat or fatty bacon	A sprig of savory, chopped
Salt and pepper	1tbsp chopped parsley
1tbsp wine vinegar	2 cups jellied stock
2 onions, thinly sliced	Pastry (10oz)
	Beaten egg

Joint the rabbits (remove the bones if you wish). Cut the fat or bacon into strips and insert through the flesh with a larding needle. Put into ovenproof dish with the seasoning and vinegar. Blanch the onions in boiling water, drain and add to the dish with the cloves, herbs and stock.

Cover with pastry, decorate and glaze with beaten egg. Bake at 400°F for 1 hour. Cover the pastry with foil or greaseproof paper, then lower the heat to 325°F for a further 1–2 hours.

STILL LIFE WITH CRAB

Abraham van Beyeren (c. 1620-90)

THE HAGUE (MAURITSHUIS)

One of the most fascinating details in this still life is the tiny self-portrait the artist has ingeniously painted into the reflection on the elaborate silver jug. It was a device van Beyeren used in many of his paintings as did his illustrious 15th-century predecessor Jan van Eyck.

An almost exact contemporary of Van Beyeren was a government official named Constantijn Huygens (1596-1687) who was an early champion of Rembrandt. He studied art himself with the printmaker Hondius and wrote revealingly about the art and artists of his day in his autobiography, written in Latin at the age of 33. It lay undisturbed among his papers until the 19th century.

In one passage he writes, "If nothing else, let us learn this, that the estimation which we commonly make of the size of things is variable, untrustworthy, and fatuous insofar as we believe that we can eliminate every comparison and can discern any great difference in size merely by the evidence of our senses. Let us in short be aware that it is impossible to call anything 'little' or 'large' except by comparison." This was in direct contrast to the Italian humanist view that man was the scale and measure of all things.

These views had been incompatible for more than a century. In his time, Michelangelo (1475-1564) wrote, "In Flanders they paint with a view to external exactness of such things as may cheer you and of which you cannot speak ill . . . without reason or art, without symmetry or proportion, without skillful choice or boldness and finally, without substance or vigor . . ."

The "external exactness" of which Michelangelo complained perfectly suited the newly rich Protestant, independent Dutch. The economic climate of prosperous Holland in the 17th century created an atmosphere in which artists flourished.

This painting is typical of what a rich burgher would buy with a view to investment. Everything in this picture is clearly on display. No object on which the artist has lavished his considerable skill is common or obscured. The expensive exotic fruit is cut in half or peeled to reveal its luscious interior, or at the least is pristine and fresh. There are no *memento mori* of worms or maggots here. Polished silver gleams and silver-gilt glitters. The practical Dutch patron bought visible quality. If you hung a picture like this on your walls, you were obviously doing extremely well.

Alas, the Dutch economy suffered a collapse when the French invaded in 1672 and many Dutch painters either left the country in search of richer patrons or retired from painting altogether. This Dutch recipe comes from *De Verstandige Kock of Sorghvuldige Iluyshoudster* (The Sensible Cook or the Careful Housekeeper), Marcus Doornick, Amsterdam, 1668.

TO PREPARE A DISH OF CRABS

"After the crabs have been cooked well, open the crabs and take away all the dirt. Chop parsley very fine and put it in the shell of the crab. Add pepper, mace, nutmeg and butter. Heat the crabs and stir in the shell until the contents are done. Add lemon juice or verjus."

Serves 4

2 large cooked crabs	1tbsp butter, melted
2tbsp chopped parsley	or cream
Salt and pepper	A squeeze of lemon juice
A pinch of ground mace and	
nutmeg	

Remove the claws and break the body along the natural line. With a teaspoon, scrape out all the brown meat inside the big shells. Thoroughly clean the shells and rub with a little oil for serving. Remove all the white meat from the body and claws, being careful to remove all small pieces of shell and inedible pieces. Mix the crab meat together with the parsley and seasonings, and moisten with lemon juice and a little butter or cream to taste. Spoon back into the shells and, if required hot, cover with foil. Heat through in a moderate oven, 350°F, for 10-12 minutes. This recipe is good hot or cold.

STILL LIFE WITH ORANGES

Jan Davidsz de Heem (1606–84)

PARIS (LOUVRE)

Jan Davidsz de Heem was born in 1606 in Utrecht and died in Antwerp in 1684. He was one of the greatest painters of the Baroque still life which reached its apogee in Holland in the 17th century. Several members of the de Heem family were also well-known artists: his father David, his younger brother David Davidsz, his sons Cornelis and David Jansz.

He had moved from Utrecht to Antwerp by 1636 because he said "there one could have rare fruits of all kinds, large plums, peaches, cherries, oranges, lemons, grapes and others, in finer condition and state of ripeness to draw from life . . ."

The Dutch could indulge their passion for exotic fruit as a consequence of the prosperity brought by the Dutch East India Company, which was formed in 1602 and which exercised a monopoly in the waters between the Cape of Good Hope and the Straits of Magellan until the end of the 18th century.

Oranges had been grown in Europe for several centuries before Jan de Heem placed them so prominently in this painting but they are a sub-tropical fruit and would either have been imported from a warmer country than Holland or grown in greenhouses. Consequently the orange was expensive, rare and fancy, as was the pomegranate shown next to it in the picture.

The orange is presumed to be a native of southern China and has been described as a 20-million-year-old berry. The first time oranges were mentioned outside China (and said to be costly then) was in Rome in the first century AD.

The Moors grew oranges in Spain as early as the eighth century and by the 12th century vast orchards stretched from Granada to Seville. The Saracens also cultivated them in Sicily from the 11th until the 13th centuries, and a customs list of 1332 lists them as being exported from Nice.

It became fashionable for royalty to construct orangeries. The most lavish was at Versailles, built by Mansart for Louis XIV, where 1200 orange trees grew in silver tubs. The oranges for the King's table, however, were imported from Portugal. Frederick Augustus I, Elector of Saxony, is said to have spent so much money on building his orangery that he could not afford a palace to go with it.

Eleanor of Castile bought seven oranges from the cargo of a Spanish ship which landed in Southampton in 1200 – possibly the date they first arrived in England. They were well known enough for Shakespeare to mention them and by the time Charles II was on the throne "orange girls" (Nell Gwynn was one) – whose virtue was open to speculation – sold them in the theatres.

The orange now known as the Seville orange is the bitter *Citrus aurantium,* the bigard, which is probably the ancestor of all oranges. It is the only one that grows true from seed. The sweet oranges, imported by the Portuguese, which the Elizabethans called *portyngale* are known as Valencias (*Citrus sinensis*).

This recipe comes from a late 16th-century Belgian manuscript. The "orange apples" were probably a variety called "Aeght-apple," no longer available today.

TO COOK ORANGE APPLES

"Peel the orange apples and cut them in slices. Cook them in red wine with sugar, ginger powder, cinnamon powder. After cooking sprinkle with sugar and make it as sweet as you like."

Serves 8

8 large eating apples	A pinch of ground ginger
⅔ cup red wine	Grated rind of 1 orange
Heaped ½ cup brown sugar	1tbsp confectioners' sugar
A pinch of ground cinnamon	

Peel and core the apples, slice them thickly, and cook gently in the above ingredients, adding a little water if necessary. Simmer until tender (about 5 minutes). Leave to cool in the syrup. Sprinkle with confectioners' sugar.

TEA PARTY AT LORD HARRINGTON'S HOUSE

Peter Phillips (1708–1747)

NEW HAVEN (YALE CENTER FOR BRITSH ART)

The painter Peter Phillips served his patron, Lord Harrington, well with this graceful picture of the noble man, gorgeously attired, with his guests and family. They are all displaying to magnificent effect the height of "English style" so much admired across the channel. Madame de la Tour du Pin wrote at the time that, as well as adopting the English tea party, young Parisian gentlemen of fashion even attempted to speak with English accents.

The people in this group probably dined shortly before 4 o'clock in the afternoon. Then, after the long dinner was over and the tablecloth removed for dessert and wine, the ladies often, but not always, would have retired for coffee. Any gentleman who did not wish to remain in the dining room drinking joined them. Tea with cake and sandwiches would have arrived in the drawing room at around 8.30pm and with it the men who had been summoned by the butler. On formal occasions, yet another substantial meal would have been served. The party would have refreshed themselves between 10 and 11 o'clock with cold meat, a selection of hot dishes, sweets, fruit and more wine, before leaving around midnight.

The group on the left of the picture is drinking tea which was first imported from China directly to England by the East India Company. The delicate small tea bowls, teapots and sugar bowls like the dainty ones on the table were imported at the same time. They were expensive and as they were symbols of status it is not surprising that the artist has carefully included them in the picture. Tea was introduced to the English court as a fashionable drink by Catherine of Braganza, the Portuguese wife of Charles II, who was already familiar with tea when she came to England.

Thomas Twining opened his first tea shop for ladies in Devereux Court, London, in 1717. Fifteen years later Vauxhall Pleasure Gardens were turned into an enormously successful tea garden where people of all classes could mingle and enjoy concerts, spectacles and sports. By the 1740s tea was drunk by almost everybody at breakfast, with a little milk or cream, and again after dinner. Unlike the Chinese, the English always preferred their tea sweet. Tea drinking was the cause of a rise in sugar consumption in the 18th century.

Eventually other ways of using tea were found. "Tea caudles" were thought to be restorative. One 17th-century recipe calls for a quart of tea boiled with a pint of white wine, the beaten yolks of four eggs, and flavored with grated nutmeg and sugar (not unlike Christmas Egg Nog).

Tea Cream was a popular early 18th-century dessert cream. Earlier, chocolate cream had been the rage. In the 1736 edition of La Chapelle's *The Modern Cook* the chopped gizzards of two or three fowls were melted in the cream to "velvet" it; in later recipes rennet was used instead. Charles Millington's Tea Cream, adapted from *The Housekeeper's Domestic Library* (1805), is more suitable for modern tastes.

TEA CREAM

"Simmer together in a sturdy saucepan a pint of cream with 2 coriander seeds, a stick of cinnamon, a strip of lemon peel a few inches long and 3 table-spoons of sugar, for 10 minutes. Remove the peel and spices with a slotted spoon. Brew a small pot of green tea, strain and measure 5 ounces and add to the cream. Strain the lightly beaten whites of 6 eggs into the cream and tea mixture and whisk over a medium heat until it thickens. Pour into small cups or a pretty dish and leave until cold. Garnish with ratafia bisquits to serve."

Serves 6

1pt double cream	Rind of quarter of a lemon
2 coriander seeds	1/4pt China tea
1 cinnamon stick	6 egg whites, lightly beaten
3tbsp caster sugar	

Follow the original method.

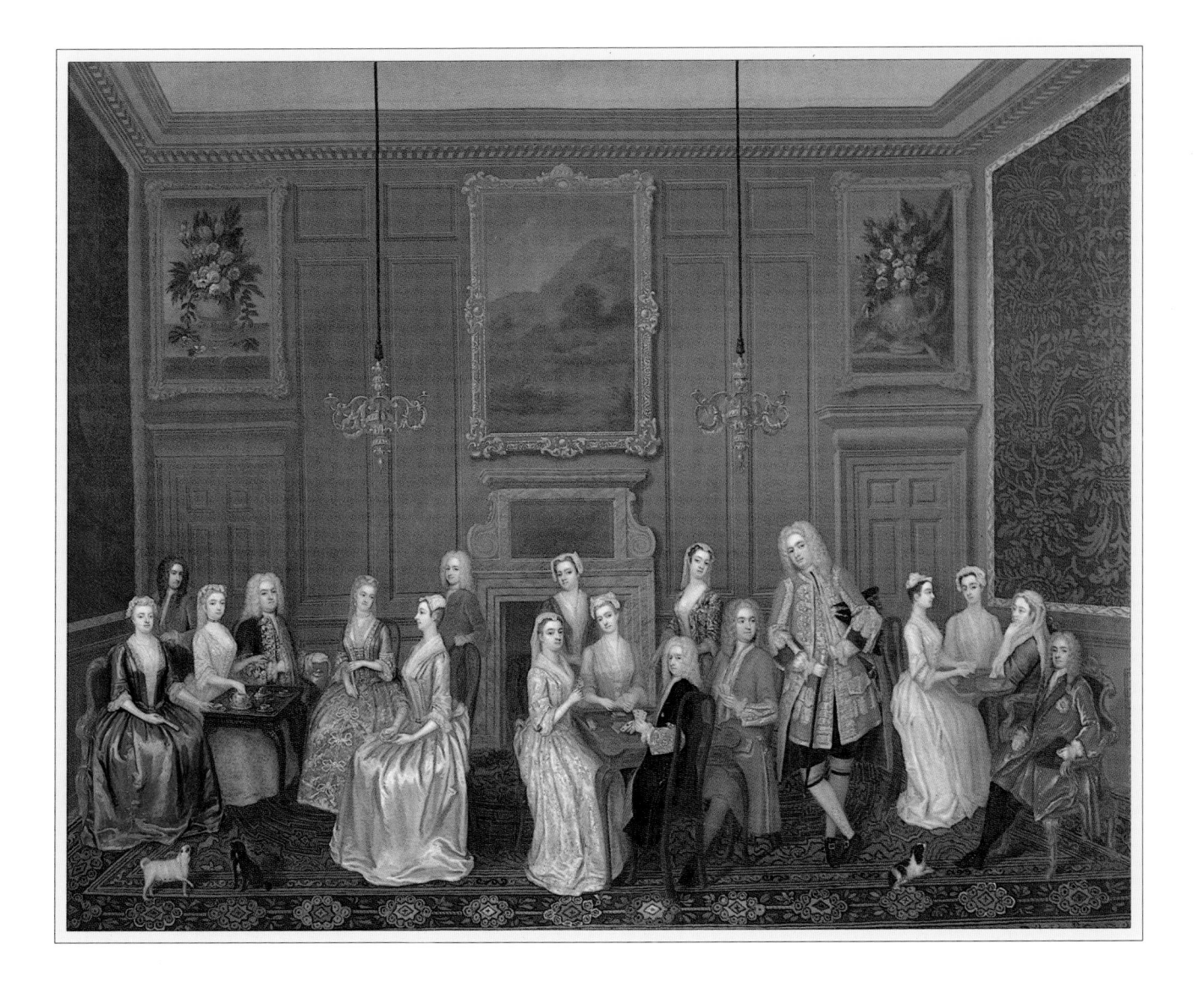

THE HUNTING LUNCHEON

Carle van Loo (1705–65)

PARIS (LOUVRE)

Carle van Loo and his elder brother Jean-Baptiste, who brought him up and taught him to paint, came from a family of Flemish origin. They both spent time in Rome but Carle returned to Paris in 1724 and won first prize in the French Academy competition. After another sojourn in Italy, he returned again to Paris in 1734 and became a professor at the Academy in 1737. In 1763 he was elected director and was appointed first painter to King Louis XV. He and François Boucher were the darlings both of Paris society and the foreign courts; Madame de Pompadour commissioned him to work for her at her château at Bellevue. Van Loo is best known for his stylish Rococo portraits of European royalty and genre scenes of the nobility at play. Even though his paintings are now seen as facile and not terribly original, he influenced a number of other painters.

This painting is a typical example of van Loo's work, displaying his noble patrons enjoying their favorite pastime. But there was a darker picture looming behind this pretty scene of aristocrats relaxing over their luncheon. Neither the painter nor the cheerful lords and ladies he painted ever gave a thought to the devastation and misery the lavish hunting parties caused the peasant population. The hunt was regarded as a sacred ritual by the nobility and the scourge of agriculture by the peasants.

As Sanche de Gramont wrote in *Epitaph for Kings*, an account of the decline of the French monarchy and the advent of the Revolution, "For the nobility, the first function of the land was not to be tilled, but to serve as a course over which men on horseback chased fleeing animals. Hunting privileges, against which there was no recourse, did more damage than all other feudal abuses combined."

Not only were the peasants' crops continually threatened by hunters galloping pell-mell over the land, but if there were pheasants or partridge on it they had to let it lie fallow to allow them to breed undisturbed. They were not allowed to own dogs, were required to plant thorny bushes to provide cover for game and were forbidden to build fences or hedges that would stop the precious game from ruining their fields. Domestic animals were often ruthlessly slaughtered if they got in the way of hunters. Tenant farmers were even less fortunate as they were not allowed to weed or remove trees from the land they rented and had to ensure that plowing, planting and harvesting did not coincide with hunting.

The penalties for poaching game were severe. In England in 1217 two years after the signing of Magna Carta it was decreed that "none shall lose life or limb for pursuing the King's game." It *was* a capital offense at various times in the succeeding centuries and as late as 1816 anyone caught with a net or stick who was judged to have been abroad with the intent to take game or rabbits could be transported for seven years. In 1880 tenants for the first time were given rights to shoot the rabbits and hares destroying their crops.

This recipe comes from Menon's *La Cuisinière bourgeoise*.

SAUCE PIQUANTE

"Shred some salad herbs very fine with half a clove of garlic and 2 shallots, dilute the whole with a little mustard, sweet oil, a dash of vinegar, salt and pepper."

HERB DRESSING

2tbsp mixed chopped fresh herbs (parsley, chives, thyme, etc)	½tsp French-style mustard
1 small clove garlic, crushed	Salt and pepper
2 small shallots, finely chopped	¼ cup walnut, hazelnut, almond or olive oil
1tbsp vinegar	

Mix all the ingredients thoroughly together, season to taste. Use for salads and cold meat dishes.

DINNER AT THE PRINCE OF CONTI'S

Michel Ollivier (1712–84)

PARIS (LOUVRE)

This elegant supper party was given by the Prince de Conti, the Grand Prior of the Knights of Malta, at the Temple where he and his family lived. Sixteen years later on August 13, 1792, King Louis XVI, Queen Marie Antoinette and their children were moved to the Temple and imprisoned there. The King made his final journey from it to the guillotine on January 2, 1793.

Suppers similar to the happy event depicted in this painting were described by Madame de la Tour du Pin. Born Henrietta-Lucy Dillon, in Paris in 1770, she wrote her memoirs between 1820 and 1853. Recalling her youth before the French Revolution, from which she narrowly escaped to America, she wrote:

"In those days, it was not the custom to give great dinner parties, for people dined early: at half-past two and three o'clock at the latest. By dinner time the ladies would sometimes have their hair dressed but they would still be in *déshabillé* . . . After dinner, people conversed; sometimes we played a game of backgammon. Then the ladies would go off to dress and the gentlemen would wait to accompany them to the theater, if they were to be in the same box. If one stayed at home after dinner, there was a continuous stream of visitors. Supper guests did not arrive until half-past nine. Socially that was the really important hour of the day. There were two kinds of supper. Those given by people whose supper table was open to guests on every day of the week so that people could come when they wished, and those to which one was invited, which were numerous and brilliant. I am speaking of the days when I was a child, that is to say, between 1778 and 1784. All the toilettes, all the elegance, everything that the beautiful, fashionable society of Paris could offer in refinement and charm was to be found at these suppers."

One of the dishes shown on the table is a pyramid of fruit. Such pyramids were fashionable from 1650 until the end of the 18th century. The food, usually fruit, could be stuck together with caramel or placed in a mold and chilled. Another method was to stack the fruit carefully in a tin funnel which was then turned out onto a porcelain dish, and yet another was to stack portions of the pyramid on graduated sized dishes. Madame de Sévigné, who seems to have spent most of her life writing lively letters vividly describing the fashions, foibles and personalities of 17th-century life, mentions one supper party where the pyramid was too high and "twenty porcelains were completely overturned at the door, the noise of which silenced the violins, oboes and trumpets."

Desserts made with cream were popular, and there are several recipes for them in the 1776 edition of Menon's *Les Soupers de la Cour. Mousse a la Creme* or Whipped Cream was scented with "a few drops of Bergamote-water (or of Cedar)" and orange flower water. An authentic flavor of the 18th century can be achieved by making Marmalade Cream using Twining's special Earl Grey Marmalade. It contains oil of bergamot, which gives Earl Grey tea its distinctive aroma.

MOUSSE A LA CREME

"Boil a pint of Cream, and mix it with a few spoonfuls of any sort of marmalade, and a little dried preserved lemon chopped very fine; When it is but just Milk-Warm, put some Rennet to turn it, and serve it with good plain Cream and pounded Sugar over it."

MARMALADE CREAM DESSERT

Serves 6

2½ cups light cream	2tsp chopped candied peel
3tbsp marmalade	Rennet (as advised on package)

To serve

⅔ cup heavy cream	2tbsp superfine sugar

Follow the original recipe but use the relevant amount of rennet advised by the manufacturer for the quantity of the liquid.

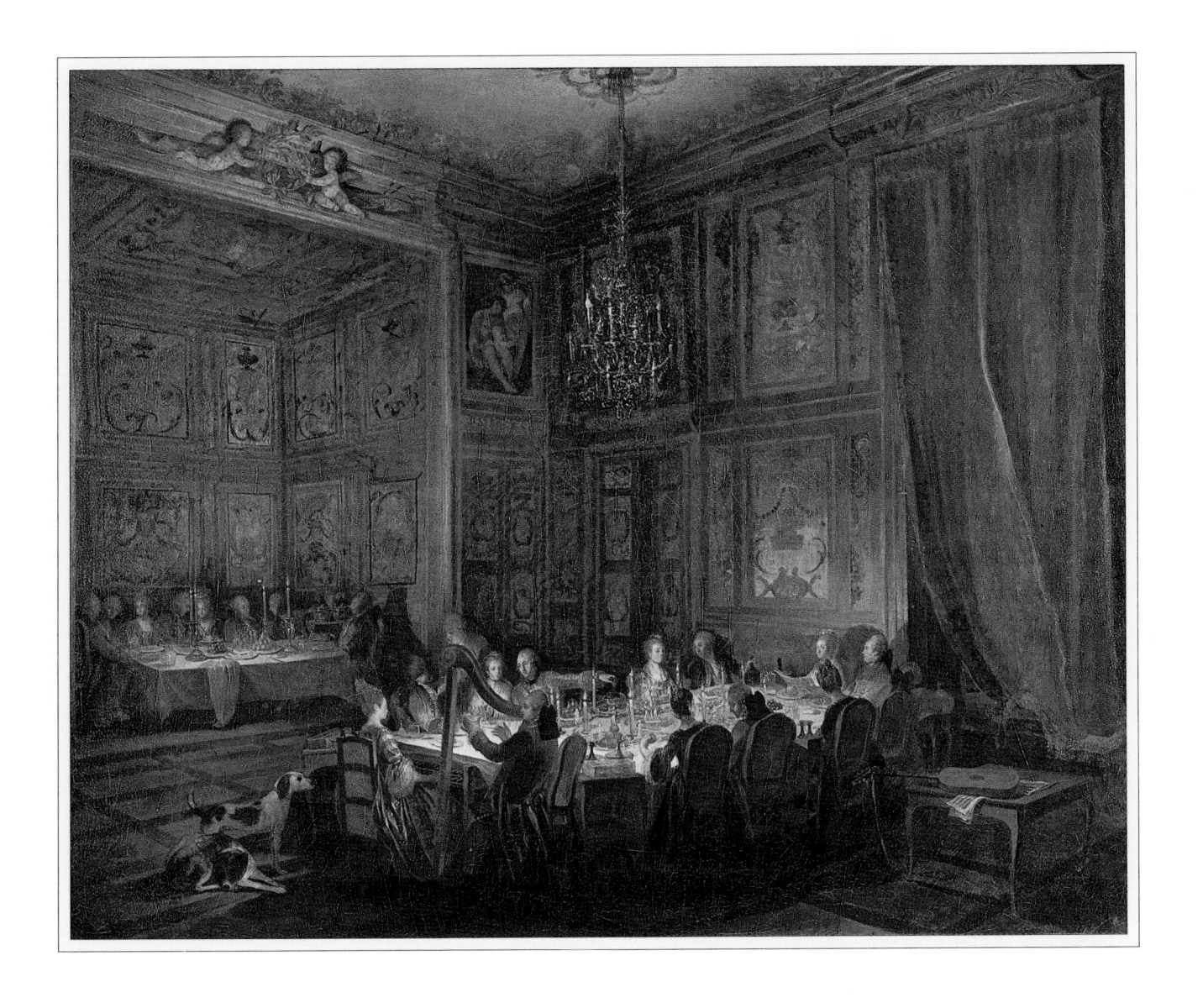

PRINCE LUDWIG AT THE INN

Catel

The human animal clearly has a deep-seated need to travel. Even when it was no longer necessary to search for food and fresh pasture, people with means were on the move. The medieval pilgrim satisfied this urge and cloaked it with piety by visiting as many shrines as possible and proudly wearing a badge to prove it. The adventurer with wander-lust could go on a crusade, which combined avarice with the sanctimonious ambition to free the holy lands from the grip of the infidel. Rape, pillage, seizure of territory and lucrative trade were additional rewards for the egregiously high-minded crusaders.

In later centuries the religious aspect was transmuted into a quest for experience, knowledge and general broadening. For some, wagon-loads of exotic trophies were shipped back to dazzle stay-at-homes. The Grand Tour was an essential part of a gentle person's education.

Italy was one of the most popular destinations and Prince Ludwig of Bavaria and his merry companions in the picture are enthusiastically sampling the wine in an Italian inn. They appear to be content with the meal on the table, unlike Charles Burney whose recollections of his travels in the 18th century are among the many quoted by Christopher Hibbert in his book, *The Grand Tour*. Describing his journey across the Ligurian Apennines, Burney wrote, "At length, about eleven at night, we arrived at a wretched inn or pigsty, half stable and half cowhouse, with a fire but no chimney, surrounded by boors and muleteers, all in appearance cut-throat personages, with no kind of refreshment but cold veal and stinking eggs." Another Englishman, Craufurd Tait Ramage, who was tutor to the sons of the British Consul in Naples, complained about traveling in the Kingdom of the Two Sicilies of the "everlasting sausage, coarse black bread and miserable wine . . . cold salted fish, swimming in vapid vinegar." Quail or *beccafico*, a cup of coffee with the liqueur, *rosolio*, made from figs, an omelet, soup and a plate of macaroni in a monastery were rare pleasures.

The gentlemen in the painting may have enjoyed a meal more like the one in Milan which pleased the traveler, Adam Walker, "plump fowls, tolerable boiled beef, and the delicious small birds called *Becchia Fecchi*; and for the first time since we entered Italy, had a boat of melted butter to our greens. This was a great treat . . . At the better inns we seldom sit down to less than a dozen dishes (half of which we cannot eat) and a dessert of peaches, pears, and delicious grapes . . . The fish from the Mediterranean are very good – fine lobsters, plaice, sardines, mullets, etc . . . I never saw such large and beautiful apples, melons, pompions (pumpkins), nor such quantities and variety of fine grapes."

This recipe for *Crostini* comes from *L'arte della cucina*, written in the 18th century, by Don Felice Libera. The travelers whose journals are quoted may have been given it at the better inns. *Crostini* are still popular in Italy, often now made with chicken livers, or with tiny shellfish if you are by the seaside.

CROSTINI DI PROSCIUTTO

"Take slices of ham and cut into cubes. Put some butter in a casserole and onto the fire. Add the ham and chopped sage and fry. Add some sugar and a little vinegar, and boil together. Taste to see if it is to your liking, neither too sweet nor too sharp. Mix a little flour with water and add enough to the sauce to make it not too liquid or too thick. When the sauce has reached perfection pour it onto slices of bread fried in butter and send it to the table hot."

ITALIAN HAM

¼lb cooked ham, sliced	1tbsp vinegar
1tbsp butter	2tsp cornstarch
A pinch of chopped sage	2tbsp water
1tsp sugar	Ground black pepper

Cut the ham into cubes. Melt the butter in a pan, add the ham, sage, sugar and vinegar. Mix the cornstarch and water together and add, stir until thickened, simmer for a minute then serve on fried bread or toast.

March *from* The Month of the Year *by Robert Furber,*
1732
Victoria & Albert Museum, London.

CHAPTER THREE

THE
BOUNTY OF
NATURE

The raw ingredients that have

inspired cooks and artists alike over

the centuries

THE FRUIT SELLER

Vincenzo Campi (1536–91)

MILAN (GALLERIA BRERA)

This exquisite still life in a landscape by the Italian painter, Vincenzo Campi (1536–91), is a fusion of several artistic threads which were often woven into Italian painting in the 16th century. From the middle of the century, Venice had been a center of art where Italian and Flemish schools of painting came into close contact, as painters from the north came to study in Italy.

Vincenzo Campi, who had been to Spain where there was a strong tradition of still-life painting, was a painter of the Mannerist school. Mannerism developed as a revolt against the religious and historical themes of classical idealism, and introduced new subjects – among them the novelty and, as one art historian has described it, "the vulgar reality of shops and food displays."

The sheer beauty of fruit, freed from the iconographic strictures of the past, played a prominent role in the new Mannerist pictures. Fruit had, of course, always been an important element in the human diet from the earliest times.

Charlemagne, who became King of the Franks in 768 AD, and was crowned Emperor of the West in 800 AD, sent to his officers a garden list of plants to be grown throughout his vast realm. It included seven types of apple, five varieties of pear, plums of various species, crab apples, medlars, peaches of various kinds, quinces, mulberries, figs, cherries, as well as flowers: lilies, roses, hollyhocks, mallows, gladioli, poppies and heliotropes, together with herbs for medicinal and culinary purposes.

In Milan in 1368, at the wedding banquet for Lionel, Duke of Clarence (third son of Edward III), and Violante, daughter of Bernabo Visconti of Milan, each of the 18 courses was accompanied by an elaborate gift. The last course was simply listed as "fruit" and the gift that went with it two great coursers (hunting dogs) called Lion and Abbot that belonged to Visconti.

The recipe here is taken from *L'Arte della Cucina* (see page 36).

TORTA DE PERA

"Take pears of good quality, peel and cut in thin slices. Put in a brass pan with a little water with some sugar already dissolved in it. Cook on the fire till the water is consumed, stirring all the time so it does not stick. Pour onto a plate and cool. Spread some *pasta sfragola* over a buttered tart pan and strew over some ground almonds, sugar, powdered cinnamon and finely chopped lemon peel. Then a layer of the pear, followed by the almond mixture, followed by the pear, followed by the almond mixture again.

At last put on some strips of butter and cover with a layer of pastry and bake in the oven. When cooled, dust with sugar and serve."

PEAR TART

Serves 8

1½lb pears, peeled and cored	½ cup almonds, ground
	3tbsp sugar
2tbsp water	¼tsp ground cinnamon
2tbsp superfine sugar	Finely grated rind of 1 lemon

For the pasta sfragola

6tbsp butter	1 egg yolk
1½ cups fine semolina	2tbsp rose water, water
6tbsp superfine sugar	or milk
A pinch of salt	

For the pastry topping
6oz piecrust dough

Slice the pears thinly, put into a pan with the water and sugar. Cook until the pears are soft and the liquid absorbed. Mix the ground almonds, sugar, cinnamon and lemon rind together. Set aside.

Make the *pasta sfragola*; cut the butter into the semolina and add the remaining ingredients to make a soft, pliable dough. Press neatly into a well-greased 8 in diameter pie-plate. Sprinkle over a thin layer of the ground almond mixture, then a layer of the cold pear purée. Then another layer of almonds and a layer of pear purée; finish with a layer of almonds. Dot the top with a knob of butter. Roll out pastry to cover the top. Brush with a little beaten egg and bake at 375°F for 35–45 minutes. Cool and dust with sugar.

LANDSCAPE WITH MAN AND FOOD

attributed to Giovanna Garzoni (1600–1670)

FLORENCE (PALATINA GALLERY)

It is easy to see why Garzoni's miniature portraits of flowers, fruit and vegetables, people and even dogs were collected so avidly by her noble patrons. Painstakingly executed in delicate tempera, they manage to be full-blooded yet refined. She was not held in such esteem by her grander contemporaries who painted historical, religious and imaginative large-scale works. When she died in 1670, the exquisite art of the miniaturist was also dying and Garzoni herself was soon forgotten.

From the documents she left, it is evident that she worked all over Italy. In 1642 she and her brother went to Rome and in October of that year she went to Florence, where again her patrons were the ruling Medici and the most exalted members of Florentine society. She worked for the Grand Duke of Tuscany and his family. Cardinal Giovan Carlo di Medici and his brother, Leopoldo, were among her most important clients and it was for the former she painted a portrait of Cardinal Richelieu, recently discovered in the Uffizi, which is mentioned in her records. The Grand Duchess of Tuscany, Vittoria della Rovere, had in her favorite villa, Poggio Imperiale, a collection of 40 paintings by Garzoni. Among them is an enchanting portrait of a pop-eyed lapdog on a table, with a Chinese teacup and two pieces of bread (one with two startlingly life-like flies on it), that now hangs in the Pitti Palace in Florence.

Her subjects were not always as straightforward as they appear to us. They incorporated a symbolism her patrons were familiar with: a composition which included a carnation, for example, was a visual reference to chastity; a butterfly referred to imprudence, a tulip in full bloom represented death, and a serpent stood for evil. Giovanna Garzoni also imbued a simple composition of fruit or flowers with a depth of feeling and acute observation and harmony of composition which transcended the merely decorative.

According to Silvia Meloni, some of the attributions on the inventory of the Poggio Imperiale are less certain than those of the 1675 inventory of Leopoldo's estate, which indicate that its author knew Garzoni's work well. By the time the Grand Duchess Vittoria died, the inventory entry on this picture read "said to be done in the hand of a Giovanna Garzoni from Lucca" and it is possible that this curious picture, though it displays something less than the clarity, sureness and refinement of other works known to be by her hand, may have been correctly attributed.

It is however, an appealing picture and the food in it is just as familiar in Italy today as it would have been in the century in which it was painted.

The recipe here is taken from *La Nuovissima Cucina Economica* (see page 40).

INSALATINE ALLA GENOVESE

"Cut the cooked ham (or meat, fish or salami) into cubes and add some capers, small pieces of broccoli, cauliflower or cubes of asparagus, zucchini, green beans or other cooked vegetables already dressed in a vinaigrette (oil, vinegar, salt, pepper and mustard); unite with a chopped hard-boiled egg, shrimp tails and anything else such as de-stoned olives, fried calamari, oysters blanched in their water, and several fillets of fried tongue. Mix all well together and fill a box of fried bread and serve at once . . ."

GENOESE SALAD

Serves 4

²⁄₃ cup cubed cooked ham	1¹⁄₃ cups broccoli flowerettes
²⁄₃ cup sliced and cut in strips salami	1¹⁄₃ cups cauliflower flowerettes
7oz canned shrimps in brine, drained	1¹⁄₃ cups beans or asparagus or sliced zucchini
4oz canned smoked mussels or oysters	4 hard-boiled eggs, chopped
1tbsp capers	12 pitted olives
	²⁄₃ cup vinaigrette dressing

Lightly cook any vegetables *al dente*, rinse and drain well and allow to cool. Put all the ingredients together in a large bowl and toss with dressing. Croutons of fried bread can be added just before serving.

STILL LIFE WITH PLUMS AND MELON

Pierre Dupuis (1610–82)

Pierre Dupuis, who painted this enticing basket of glowing summer fruits and a melon, was probably in Italy between 1630 and 1640. This picture shows the Italian influence that predominates in his paintings during that time. His work is, however, absolutely typical of French still-life painting of the middle of the 17th century. His later paintings, such as the one he exhibited at the Salon in 1673, had the popular Flemish subject of a monkey in a still life.

Dupuis was admitted to the French Academy in 1663, along with several other flower and animal painters, including the first woman painter to become an academician, Catherine Duchemin (the flower painters Geneviève and Madeleine de Boulogne were admitted in 1669 and Catherine Perrot in 1682). Dupuis must have had an international reputation as his paintings were in the celebrated collection of the Archduke Leopold Wilhelm of Austria.

The melon was still relatively new to France when Dupuis painted it – it probably arrived there at the end of the 15th century. In 1583 Professor Jacques Pons, Dean of the College of Doctors in Lyons, wrote a learned treatise on melons and listed 50 different ways of eating them. They were served as hors d'oeuvres, chilled and sprinkled with sugar or salt and pepper; cooked; in soups and fritters, and in compôtes which could even include the peel.

Melons originally came from the Middle East, most probably from Persia. They have been known since ancient times; the earliest mention of them appears to be in the epic of Gilgamesh, a legendary King of Sumeria in the third century BC; they are also mentioned in the Bible as one of the foods that the Hebrews missed (the others were fish and cucumbers) when they were wandering in the desert after leaving Egypt. Melons were grown in Ur and an Assyrian herbal lists them. Pliny wrote about them in the first century AD, Galen in the second and a third-century Roman gardening manual gives directions for growing them. Charlemagne listed them and Marco Polo said that the city of Shibarghan in Afghanistan "had the best melons in the world in very great quantity" and described how they were sliced and sun-dried "when they become sweeter than honey." Jean de la Quintinie, Louis XIV's gardener-in-chief, grew seven varieties for him under glass at Versailles.

The recipe below comes from a 17th-century cookbook, *Le Patissier François*.

SUMMER FRUIT PIE

"Line your pie dish with a layer of fine or flaky pastry; sprinkle some sugar over it, then fill with topped redcurrants or crab-apples, or ripe cherries, or halves of apricot or peeled and stoned plums. If you prefer to use whole apricots you should peel them first. Add a knob of butter, a little ground cinnamon, some thin slices of candied lemon peel and a handful of sugar or more, depending on the size of the pie. Cover the pie with a layer of pastry which can be scored in the center, then glaze it and place it in the oven; when it is cooked, sprinkle sugar over the top, put it back in the oven for a short while, and then it will be ready."

½lb shortcrust or flaky pastry	½oz butter
3tbsp caster sugar	1tsp ground cinnamon
1lb summer fruit, prepared as necessary	Rind of ¼ lemon, in thin strips
	Milk to glaze

Divide the pastry in two, roll out thinly and line a 20-cm/8-in pie dish with half of it. Sprinkle sugar on the base, fill with chosen fruit, add butter, and cover with remaining pastry. Make slits in centre. Seal the edges of the pastry, brush with milk and place in centre of a hot oven 200°C/400°F/Gas 6) for 20 minutes. Lower to 170°C/325°F/Gas 3 and cook until filling is soft (another 10 to 20 minutes depending on the fruit).

BROAD BEANS

Giovanna Garzoni (1600–70)

FLORENCE (PITTI PALACE)

Looking at this enchanting portrait of the humble broad bean, the "meat of the poor," it is easy to understand why Giovanna Garzoni was that rare creature – a successful, unmarried woman artist. She earned a fortune as a miniaturist and it was in that form, using tempera on vellum, that she executed these homely beans. She left her considerable estate to the Accademia di San Lucca and, apparently, an album of flower and insect studies. Although a few of her paintings have survived and are in the collections of the Palazzo Pitti and the Uffizi in Florence, the album is lost, as Germaine Greer wrote in *The Obstacle Race* – her book about women artists.

The broad bean, *Vicia faba*, a member of the pea family, has been eaten since prehistoric times – they have been found (in carbonized form) in Iron Age sites in Europe and Britain. It was the most important bean in Europe until the discovery of the New World and was a staple food in the diet of the poor.

An inherited allergy to broad beans, called favism, which occurs among people in the Mediterranean basin where the bean originated, may account for the fact that the ancient Greeks and Romans associated it with bad luck or even death, and avoided it in religious ritual. The priests of Jupiter in Rome were forbidden to touch broad beans or even mention the word *faba*.

In Rome beans were used as counters in elections and if you were advised to "abstain from beans" it was a warning to steer clear of politics.

Beans and other legumes and even acorns were made into bread when cereal crops were poor or failed entirely, which happened with agonizing regularity. In the ninth century AD "grievous famines" which sometimes lasted three or four years afflicted Europe 20 times. Bean bread, rank and heartily despised though it was, was still being used in times of dearth until the middle of the 18th century.

Broad beans, like many other foods which may once have been the salvation of a starving population, seem to satisfy an atavistic longing in gourmets for real food. A fashionable restaurant in Rome today, for example, proudly serves its celebrated Tuscan bean soup – a simple peasant dish which has been a comforting winter food for centuries.

When broad beans are young and fresh in the spring, they are delicious even eaten raw. The mature beans are also dried for use in the winter. They can also be puréed, with the skins removed to make them more digestible, and recipes for bean purées are among the oldest in Italy.

The following recipe comes from *L'Arte della Cucina* (see page 36).

BROAD BEANS WITH HERBS

"De-pod broad beans and half cook in salted water and drain. Make a mixture of onion, parsley and marjoram and cook gently in butter. Add the beans and fry gently with a little salt and spices. Add some good broth and cook well. When ready to send to the table add two yolks beaten into a little grated cheese from Lodi."

Serves 8

2lb fava beans, shelled	Salt and pepper
1 medium onion, finely chopped	2 pinches grated nutmeg
2tbsp butter	2/3 cup stock
3tbsp chopped parsley	2 egg yolks
1tbsp chopped marjoram	2tbsp grated Parmesan (similar to Lodi)

Cook the beans in boiling, salted water for 6–8 minutes until tender. Drain well. Cook the onion in the butter until soft, add the herbs, seasoning, beans and stock. Cover and simmer for 10 minutes. Remove from the heat and stir in the egg yolks and Parmesan cheese. Serve at once.

THE APPLE-PEELER

Gabriel Metsu (1629–67)

PARIS (LOUVRE)

Gabriel Metsu was born in Leyden in Holland, but lived and worked mostly in Amsterdam. He studied with Gerard Dou and was an exact contemporary of Jan Vermeer and Gerard Ter Borch. These painters were *fijnschilder* (fine painters) as opposed to *kladschilder* (rough painters). Svetlana Alpers explains in her book on 17th-century Dutch painting, *The Art of Describing*, that "cost was often calculated according to finish: time was devoted to execution not to invention." The highly finished detailed virtuosity of their work was expensive. Dou or Vermeer could charge 600 guilders for a painting when a few years earlier an inexpensive work could be bought for less than ten.

The clients who could afford to buy their paintings from art galleries (they were seldom commissioned) appear as subjects of the paintings which they hung on their walls as decoration. They were the letter writers and spinet players, shown in their tastefully furnished, spotlessly clean and tidy interiors, discreetly lit by the soft glow of affluence. These clients also bought paintings of familiar "genre" subjects such as this kitchen maid, neatly dressed and fair of face, peeling apples – a dead rabbit artfully arranged beside her.

Both apples and rabbits were known in prehistoric times. Apples have been found in the earliest lake settlements in Switzerland and the imprint of an apple seed was found in a fossil from a neolithic site in England. Rabbits may have been native to Spain and the Balearics or north-west Africa, but were discovered in both Eastern and Western hemispheres.

There are many legends associated with apples but the Golden Apples of the Hesperides (the Canary Islands) that caused so much trouble in Greek mythology and were responsible for starting the Trojan War were, in reality, probably oranges or lemons. Horace advised picking apples by the light of the waning moon. The fertility ceremony of apple wassailing of Twelfth Night in England, which goes back to pagan times, and involves drinking quantities of cider, has recently been revived by the cider industry.

Many apple-lovers lament the scarcity of the older varieties – unsuitable for mass marketing – which are superior to most of the modern apples. In America there are still some fruit-bearing trees that were planted by the American folk hero, John Chapman, better known as Johnny Appleseed, who was born in Loominster, Massachusetts, in 1774. And there actually was a Granny Smith – an elderly widow who found a wild apple growing on her farm in Queensland, Australia.

This recipe comes from *The Sensible Cook or Careful Housekeeper* published in 1668 in Amsterdam.

TO STEW RABBITS

"Wash and clean the rabbits and tie the head between the legs. Take two cups of water and one cup of vinegar, crushed pepper, cloves and nutmeg and stew the rabbits here in. Some people also add onions. (When the rabbits are done) take a crushed rusk or grated white bread to bind the cooking liquid, and finally add a good piece of butter."

RABBIT CASSEROLE

Serves 6

2 young rabbits, skinned and jointed	¾lb onions, sliced
2½ cups water	2 cups fresh white bread
⅔ cup wine or cider vinegar	crumbs
Ground black pepper	2tbsp butter
2 large pinches of ground cloves and nutmeg	2tsp sugar

Put the rabbits into a casserole with the water, vinegar, pepper, cloves, nutmeg and onions. Cover and cook gently for about an hour until tender. Remove rabbit from liquid and put into a serving dish. Add the bread crumbs and butter to the pan, then purée until smooth. Return to the casserole and season to taste; add a little sugar if too tart. Pour over the rabbit and serve.

STILL LIFE WITH ASPARAGUS

Louise Moillon (c. 1609-96)

CHICAGO (ART INSTITUTE)

Louise Moillon, one of the few women artists in this book, appears to have worked in France between 1620 and 1674. She was primarily a still-life painter but works attributed to her do sometimes contain figures. Her still lifes are calm and slightly sombre, more in the Spanish tradition than the more exuberant Flemish masters of the period.

The Flemish were not only great painters of food but the first serious market gardeners in northern Europe. By the early 15th century the gardens outside Amsterdam were famous for salad plants. The French followed their example and by the middle of the 16th century little lettuces were grown in France even in winter.

The glowing asparagus in the front of the painting would have been something of a rarity in Louise Moillon's day. It had been rather neglected since the first century AD when the Roman writer Pliny the Elder described it as something only the rich could possibly afford.

Asparagus was introduced into the English vegetable garden in the 16th or 17th century but reached the height of its popularity in France when Louis XIV's gardening genius, Jean de la Quintinie, planted asparagus beds at Versailles. The Sun King enjoyed fresh asparagus as well as artichokes and strawberries all year round. *Asparagus officinalis,* of which there are more than 40 modern varieties, is a member of the lily family.

The recipe here comes from *Le Cuisinier François,* written by La Varenne, the *chef de cuisine* of the Marquis d'Uxelles. It was one of the most important French cookbooks of the 17th century and a best-seller. It was translated into English as *The French Cook* (published in 1653, 1654 and 1673); an Italian version, *Il Cuco Francese,* was published in 1695, 1728, 1802 and 1815; and a German version *Der Französische Koch* appeared in 1665.

ASPERGES A LA CREME

"Cut them into small pieces, not leaving anything but the green. Sauté them with fresh butter or melted lard, parsley, chives, or a bouquet. After this simmer them slowly with fresh cream and serve them if you like with a little nutmeg."

ASPARAGUS WITH CREAM

Serves 4

¾lb asparagus spears	1tbsp snipped chives
2tbsp butter	⅔ cup heavy cream
2tbsp chopped fresh parsley	Grated nutmeg

Trim the coarse ends from the asparagus and cut the spears into 1-in pieces. Heat the butter in a heavy bottomed pan and add the asparagus and herbs. Fry gently for 5 minutes to soften. Stir in the cream and simmer very gently until just tender. Sprinkle with nutmeg and serve.

STILL LIFE WITH CABBAGE AND PUMPKIN

Juan Sanchez Cotan (1561–1627)

SAN DIEGO (MUSEUM OF ART)

All of the surviving works by the Carthusian friar Juan Sanchez Cotan were probably painted before 1603 when the painter was around 40. He took holy orders that year and before he entered the monastery made an inventory of all his worldly goods. He listed 11 still lifes, including this one, which the art historian Charles Sterling calls "one of the masterpieces of Spanish painting." It was in Philadelphia in 1820 and was certainly known to the American artist Raphaelle Peale.

The Spanish still-life painters were influenced by Caravaggio (1571–1610) but Sterling writes "With the Spaniards we feel an unrelenting tension between light and shade, between the object and its setting, between the passion of the senses and the rigor of the mind." All of Sanchez Cotan's still lifes, he states, "consist of simple, wholesome food standing on a sill or held in air by the hand of a geometer and poet adept at ordering a world of marvels: did he not suspend a quince and a cabbage at the end of a string, where they turn and glow like planets in a boundless night?"

The recipes below come from relatively recent cookbooks which include original Spanish recipes. Luis Ripoll's *Llibre de Cucina Mallorquina* quotes a recipe for a "White Dish of Pumpkin" from Mestre Robert who was the cook of the King of Naples, Serenissim Senyor Don Ferran, in 1568.

"You will take the pumkins, the whitest you can find and you will boil them in water. As soon as it starts boiling take them out and put them in a clean cloth. Then you make milk of almonds for the amount of pumkin you have boiled. You will have to press them hard to bring out all the water. In an earthen pot you will put the almond milk and the pumkin and put sugar to the amount you like, onto the fire. Before putting in the pumkins you have to whip up the fire so it boils quickly and make sure you stir them from the bottom as if you were making paste. When you understand that they are well undone, let them cook a little bit more and then add rosewater and take them off the fire. Prepare the bowls, putting in each one fine sugar."

Colomba Abrinas Vidal's recipe for Quince Liquor comes from her *Cocina Selecta Mallorquina*, which she dictated when she was 80 years old.

LICOR DE CODONY O MEMBRILLO

"Peel and chop quinces and mince (you can do it with a meat mincer) and of the juice take 4 cups in a pot and 2 cups of alcohol. Put 4 cups of sugar, 1 lemon chopped, a little bit of vanilla. Put all together, when the sugar has melted, put it in a carafe and cover. You leave it for 11 days stirring once a day. When that time is passed, filter through paper filters and put it in bottles well stoppered."

QUINCE LIQUOR

Makes 2 large jars

3lb quinces, cored	*1 lemon, chopped*
2 cups brandy	*Small vanilla bean, split*
2½ cups sugar	

Put the ground fruit in a large bowl or earthenware crock with the rest of the ingredients. Stir thoroughly to dissolve the sugar. Cover and leave for 11 days, then filter and bottle. You can put in more sugar and more alcohol but not less.

SUMMER
Francesco Zucchi (1570–1627)
(PRIVATE COLLECTION)

Francesco Zucchi, who painted this exuberant representation of summer, was working in the fantastic style best known in the paintings of Guiseppe Arcimboldo (1527–93). They were hugely popular for a time, although they became unfashionable and thought to be merely decorative (the *Penguin Dictionary of Art and Artists* says they were overrated then and now). But they are now sought after by some and are claimed as the ancestors of Surrealism.

In the year Zucchi was born, 1570, Bartolomeo Scappi's *Opera*, one of the most important and influential early Italian cookbooks was published in Venice. Very little is known about his life except that he was probably Venetian, was employed by Cardinal Lorenzo Campeggi, organized a banquet in honour of Charles V, Emperor of the Holy Roman Empire, and was Pope Pius V's "secret" cook. His book is divided into six parts, dealing with meat, poultry, fish, the serving of meat, the method of preparing "pastes" (pasta) and invalid cookery.

Many of the ingredients in Zucchi's painting can be found on the banquet menu, printed in Scappi's book, which he organized for the Pope (given in full on page 150). From the first course of "cold delicacies from the sideboard" there are listed simply, "fresh grapes." Shown from the second course of "Hot foods from the kitchen: roasts" veal sweetbreads and liver with a sauce of eggplant and quails with sliced aubergines. From the third course "Hot foods from the kitchen: boiled meats and stews" there is stuffed breast of veal, boiled and garnished with flowers and cabbage soup with sausages, and from the final course "Delicacies from the Sideboard" come quince pastries (one quince per pastry), pear tarts (the pears wrapped in marzipan), and almonds on vine leaves.

The more unusual vegetables which were appearing in the 16th century are not included in the painting. Some had been known in the ancient world but until then had been grown for ornamental purposes in gardens and seldom eaten. Among them were artichokes, mentioned by Pliny (who said they came from Sicily), and asparagus, which had been cultivated in the previous century but, like spinach and peas, was not popular in the Middle Ages. And, of course, there were the New World vegetables – tomatoes, chili peppers, haricot beans, corn and potatoes.

The *tartufali* in some of Scappi's recipes present an interesting culinary mystery. Are they the white truffles of northern Italy or potatoes? Both were known by the same name in the 16th century. They were also called "papas" (the Pope is still called *Il Papa*) and were believed to have both tonic and aphrodiasic properties; King Philip II of Spain sent them as a gift to the ailing Pope in 1565.

The following recipe comes from *L'Arte della Cucina* (see page 36).

POLENTA DI ZUCCA

"Boil the marrow in salted water and then drain and fry in 2oz of fresh butter, 2 pounded cloves, basil and salt till it becomes sauce-like.

Pour into an earthenware dish and sieve in 12oz powdered sugar, 10 egg yolks, 8oz grated cheese from Lodi and 2oz fresh butter and mix everything together. Turn into a buttered casserole. Sift over breadcrumbs and cover the top with white paper, greased on both sides, and put on the lid and cover with hot ashes. When cooked turn the polenta onto a plate and send to the table. It will taste good."

ZUCCHINI POLENTA

Serves 8

2lb zucchini, sliced	½ cup confectioners' sugar
¼ cup butter	5 egg yolks
2 large pinches ground cloves	⅔ cup grated Parmesan
A few fresh basil leaves, chopped	¾ cup fresh bread crumbs
Salt	

Follow the original method, using the ingredients above, but cover the casserole with foil and bake at 375°F for 30 minutes until set. Leave to stand for 10 minutes before serving.

STILL LIFE WITH A LEG OF MUTTON

Richard Waitt (fl. 1706-26)

EDINBURGH (NATIONAL GALLERY OF SCOTLAND)

This simple composition of cauliflower, artichokes, meat and poultry has ingredients that could be found on the dinner table of any reasonably well-off family in the British Isles in the 18th century.

A typical meal of the period eaten by the country gentry was described in a letter from a well-bred young woman thus: "A little before three we sat down to dinner which consisted of three boiled chickens at top, a very fine haunch of venison at bottom; ham on one side, a flour pudding on the other, and beans in the middle . . .'

Cookbooks of the period specified the positions on the table of individual dishes. One historian has described guests racing into the dining room to choose the best places at the table. If they wanted to sample dishes elsewhere on the table they had to change places with another guest. Ladies were at a disadvantage; John Trusler wrote in 1788, "As eating a great deal is deemed indelicate in a lady . . . it will be ill manners to help her to a large slice of meat at once, or fill her plate too full. When you have served her with meat, she should be asked what kind of vegetables she likes, and the gentleman sitting next to that dish should be requested to help her."

As Barbara Norman, the author of *Tales of the Table* (1972), writes, 18th-century guests had begun to pass dishes themselves so that it "would no longer happen that a lady invited to dinner, in order not to trouble her neighbors, would eat exclusively and completely a platter of peas for dinner because that was what happened to be within her reach."

In a letter Jane Austen wrote to her sister Cassandra in response to the suggestion of a budding romance in the neighbourhood, Jane remarked that she could 'see nothing very promising between Mr P & Miss P.T. She placed herself on one side of him at first, but Miss Benn obliged her to move up higher, & she had an empty plate, & even asked him to give her mutton twice without being attended to...'

The following recipe comes from *The Country Housewife and Lady's Director* published in 1727.

A COLLAR OF MUTTON ROASTED FROM ST EDMUND'S-BURY IN SUFFOLK

'Take a Coast of Mutton, which is the Neck and Breast together skin it in the whole Piece; then parboil it, and prepare a Mixture of Crumbs of Bread; Lemon-Peel grated, a little Pepper, Salt, Nutmeg, or sweet Marjoram Powder'd . To this, add the Yolks of six hard Eggs, beat in a Mortar, with six ounces of Butter; mix this with the other Ingredients; then take the inside of the Mutton, and cover it with this Mixture, and roll it up as close as can be, and secure it in the Roll. It must be basted with Butter, salting it every now and then, and the Gratings of Crusts of Bread should be sprinkled upon it, with the seasoning above. Serve it with strong Gravey and Lemon or Orange Juice, and garnish with Lemon and Orange sliced; or when Oysters are in season, add fry'd oysters.'

Serves 8

3lb joint of lamb, boned (shoulder or leg)	½tsp dried marjoram or basil
1½ cups fresh white bread crumbs	6 hard-boiled egg yolks
Grated rind of 1 lemon	1 cup butter
Salt and pepper	¼ cup lemon or orange juice
Grated nutmeg	Slices of orange and lemon, to garnish

Put the lamb in a large pan, cover with cold water and bring to a boil. Simmer for 15 minutes. Meanwhile, put the bread crumbs, lemon rind, salt and pepper, nutmeg, herbs and egg yolks in a bowl. Stir to mix, then spoon 4tbsp of this mixture into a separate bowl and reserve. Beat the butter into the bread crumb mixture and spread it over the meaty side of the lamb. Roll the meat and tie it tightly with string. Either spit roast or place on a wire rack over a roasting pan and cook at 375°F for 45 minutes to 1 hour. After 30 minutes, baste the meat with butter and sprinkle the rest of the bread crumb mixture over the top. Baste the joint occasionally with the buttery juices. Make a well-flavored gravy and stir in the lemon or orange juice. Garnish the lamb with orange or lemon slices.

STILL LIFE WITH APRICOTS

Jean Baptiste Siméon Chardin (1699–1779)

TORONTO (ART GALLERY)

Chardin spent all his life in the St. Germain des Pres area of Paris. He is considered to be the greatest still-life painter of the 18th century. Although his work has all the refined delicacy and grace of his age, he was a true original. It was, perhaps, fortunate that he was basically self-taught and not bound by the traditions of an academic education. His humble subjects were transformed by his genius and, as he said, "one uses color but one paints with feeling." His success was assured when he became a member of the French Academy in 1728.

Chardin's last years were shadowed by sadness. His only son committed suicide in Venice in 1767, his sight began to fail (he took up pastels which were easier on his eyes) and the new director of the Academy reduced his pension and restricted his duties with the Academy (he had been responsible for hanging the official exhibitions at the Salon since 1755). His work went out of fashion and the last years of his life were spent in almost complete obscurity. In the middle of the 19th century Chardin was rediscovered by a small group of critics and collectors, including the Goncourt brothers, Edmond and Jules.

The apricots, *Prunus armeniaca*, in this painting, are closely related to the almond (*P. amygdalus*) and thrive where the almond and the pomegranate do. Both apricots and almonds are classified as succulent fruits with nut-like kernels and both have sweet and bitter varieties. The kernels of some apricots are used as a substitute for bitter almonds in the United States where bitter almonds are banned (the toxins in both can be neutralized by roasting). Apricots taste sweet when ripe but actually contain less "usable" sugar than apples, 6 to 7 per cent.

The apricot is most likely a native of North China, where it grows wild in the hills around Peking. The Chinese cultivated it as early as 2200 BC. Some authorities think it came to the West through Armenia (hence its botanical name, *armeniaca*) via Pompey's soldiers, who were there in the first century BC. Others maintain that it was grown in the Hanging Gardens of Babylon and the "armenia" in its name derives from the Babylonian-Assyrian name for it, *armanu*. What is certain is that the Romans, but not the Greeks, knew of the apricot (they may have imported it) and that it, in common with several other foods, declined in Europe after the fall of the Roman Empire except in Spain, where the Moors cultivated it, especially in the area around Granada. Apricots were introduced into California by Spanish missionaries.

Eighteenth-century French recipes for apricot liqueurs often require distilling, something now against the law in most countries. Alice B. Toklas lived all her adult life in France and was familiar with home-made French cordials and liqueurs. In her second cookbook, *Aromas and Flavors*, first published in 1958, she gives several recipes for old-fashioned liqueurs, including the one below.

APRICOT RATAFIA

"Thirty apricots, 4 quarts white wine, 2 pounds sugar, 1 quart brandy, 3-inch stick of cinnamon. Take 30 sound apricots, cut them in half and remove the pits. Place them in an enameled pot, cover with 4 quarts very good white wine. Place the pot over medium heat. When contents commence to boil add 2 pounds sugar, 1 quart brandy and a 3-inch stick of cinnamon. Remove from heat, cover the pot and allow to infuse for four days. Then strain and filter through a paper. Bottle and cork tightly. Keep in a cool place."

Makes 7½ quarts

30 apricots, halved and stoned	5 cups brandy
5 quarts good white wine	3-in stick of cinnamon
2lb superfine sugar	

Put the apricots and wine in a large preserving pan. Bring to a boil, then add the sugar, brandy and cinnamon and remove from the heat. Cover and leave to infuse for four days. Strain the liquid through cheesecloth and discard the fruit pulp. Pour the apricot liqueur into sterilized bottles and cover. Store in a cool dry place.

CERAMIC TROMPE L'OEIL

Anon, 18th century

PARIS (MUSEE DES ARTS DECORATIFS)

The ceramic *trompe l'oeil* almonds on this amusing dish from Marseille are the kernel of the fruit of *Prunus amygdalus*, a close relative of the apricot. They are important historically and are still used in cooking more than any other nut. Almonds from the neolothic period were found in excavations underneath the Palace of Knossos and in Bronze Age storerooms at Hagia Triada on Crete. They were mentioned in ancient Anatolia, Babylon, in the Hittite chronicles, and in the Bible – Aaron's rod was an almond branch. The only other nut that is mentioned in the Bible is the pistachio.

The Romans called almonds "Greek Nuts" because they imported them from Greece even though they grew in Italy. In ancient Egypt almond oil was used as a cosmetic. Charlemagne (742–814 AD) mentions them, and the first French cookbook (*c.* 1300) has recipes using almond milk.

The Persians also used ground almonds, walnuts and pistachio nuts to thicken sweet and savory dishes and the Moguls introduced them to India.

Almonds are included in a Spanish sauce, probably Moorish in origin, which is used today in Spain, rather as Worcestershire sauce is elsewhere; it is made of olive oil, saffron, almonds, parsley and water.

The arrival of almonds in medieval European cooking via the Arabs and the Crusaders was especially useful nutritionally for Lenten dishes, when meat was forbidden, as almonds are a valuable source of protein. Almonds contain 50 per cent oil, 15 per cent protein and significant amounts of Vitamins E, B2 and B3 as well as iron, calcium, phosphorus, potassium and magnesium.

Many old recipes call for the addition of a few bitter almonds mixed in with the sweet ones for flavor. The bitter almond (*Prunus amygdalus amara*) is grown mainly in Sicily, North Africa and southern France. It is smaller than the sweet almond and has a very hard shiny shell. The strong bitter taste that indicates the presence of prussic acid (the cyanide of detective novels) develops when the crushed nut is mixed with water or saliva. Bitter almonds contain a glucoside, a nitrogenous compound related to sugar, which when acted upon by an enzyme reacts with water to form prussic (hydrocyanic) acid and benzaldehyde. It is lethal in quite small doses. Fortunately the acid is extremely volatile and vanishes into the air when heated leaving only the bitter almond flavor (benzaldehyde) which is harmless in small quantities. Roasting the nuts will also destroy the enzyme system.

The late Tom Stobart included an excellent method of dry-roasting and salting sweet almonds in *The Cook's Encyclopedia*. He suggests roasting them very slowly, and watching them constantly, till they turn a pale biscuit color and can be snapped. When they are cooled, they should be shaken, first in beaten egg white and then in very fine salt.

The following recipe for almond beignets comes from Menon's *Les Soupers de la Cour*.

BEIGNETS D'AMANDES

"Pound ½lb sweet almonds and 6 or 8 bitter ones, orange flowers, chopped lemon peel, sugar in proportion, a handful of flour and 2 or 3 egg whites; pound all together adding a few drops of water or more whites to make it of proper suppleness to roll into little balls; roll them in flour to fry as forcemeat balls, strew a little fine sugar powder upon them when ready to serve."

ALMOND BEIGNETS

Makes about 16

2 cups almonds, ground	2tbsp all-purpose flour
Finely grated rind	2–3 egg whites
of 1 lemon	Oil for shallow frying
Orange flowers (optional)	Sifted confectioners' sugar
Heaped ½ cup superfine sugar	for dusting

Mix together to a stiff paste with a few drops of water if necessary. Roll into small balls. Heat the oil and fry the almond balls, tossed in a little flour, gently until golden brown. Drain and dust with confectioners' sugar. Cool.

CHERRY MARMALADE

Carl Spitzweg (1808–85)

(PRIVATE COLLECTION)

The history and origins of marmalade, depicted here, are so complex and intriguing that the culinary historian, C. Anne Wilson, has written an entire book on the subject.

The earliest form of marmalade was used by the ancient Greeks and Romans to treat stomach, liver and kidney ailments. Dioscorides gave directions in the first century AD for peeled quinces with their seeds removed to be wedged tightly together in a vessel filled with honey. This was left for a year after which the quinces became as soft as "wine-honey" which was wine and honey boiled together into a thick syrup. From the Greek name for it *melimelon* (apple-in-honey) and the Latin *melimelum*, the Portuguese word for quince (*marmelo*), and the word for the conserve made from quinces (*marmelada*), derived.

Marmalade from Portugal arrived in England, and no doubt in other parts of Europe as well, in the first half of the 15th century. It was described around 1450 as being "comfortable for a man's body and namely for the stomach," an idea that had been borrowed from earlier Greek sources. The Portuguese were probably introduced to quince marmalade by the Moors but it is the Persians who were the first to make extensive use of sugar for preserving.

The addition of aphrodisiacs, such as eringo roots, to marmalade further enhanced its reputation as a restorative. Two recipes in *A Closet for Ladies and Gentlemen* of 1608 included eringo roots preserved in sugar (these were still being made in Suffolk, England, in the middle of the 19th century).

Another recipe in the same volume adds other aphrodisiacs in case the eringo roots are not enough on their own, and suggests "Another sort of Marmelate very comfortable and restorative to any Lord or Lady" containing ginger, cock's testicles, seeds of red nettles, rocket and a Saharan lizard, *Scincus marinus*, preserved in salt, that was imported and sold by apothecaries (Dioscorides had said it was "a great provocative to lust"). By 1727 the term "marmelet madams" had come to mean ladies of uncertain virtue.

Perhaps it is just as well that the exotic history of the harmless pot of marmalade sitting sedately on breakfast tables around the world has now largely been forgotten.

Carl Spitzweg was interested in food and wrote a little book between 1850 and 1865 which he illustrated. It was discovered and published in 1962 by F. Bruckmann in Munich. This recipe comes from it.

CHERRY MARMALADE

"To 4 pounds of sweet, juicy black cherries, without stalks and stones, 1 pound of sugar and some cinnamon and cloves. The sugar should be clarified and after that the cherries and spices are added and cooked until the juice is no longer liquid. Put the cherries into glasses and seal carefully.

Instead of 4 pounds of sweet black cherries take 3 pounds of them and 1 pound of sour cherries."

Makes 3 to 4 jars

4lb fresh ripe black cherries, stoned (or frozen cherries, already pitted)	¼–½tsp ground cinnamon
	2 large pinches ground cloves
2 cups sugar	6tbsp lemon juice

Put the cherries, sugar, spices and lemon juice into a preserving pan. Heat gently to dissolve the sugar and stir from time to time. When no longer gritty, increase the heat and boil steadily until the setting stage has been reached (about an hour). There will be very little liquid left at this stage. Transfer to sterilized jars, seal and store.

Still Life with Rhubarb, Flowers and Vegetables

James Ensor (1860–1949)

BRUSSELS (ROYAL MUSEUM)

This exuberant still life shows a less familiar side of an artist better known for his more macabre subjects – the masks and skeletons painted in a powerful Expressionist manner, before that term was in general use. He exhibited with a group of artists known as "Les XX" in 1884 but they rejected his painting, "The Entry of Christ into Brussels in 1889," and voted him out of the group. Although his father was English James Ensor lived in Ostend, after training as a painter in Brussels.

The striking pink rhubarb (*Rheum rhaponticum*) in the painting is a vegetable although it is usually cooked and eaten like fruit. It may have originally come from Tibet and there is some confusion as to how it got its name. Some say it comes from Rha, the ancient name for the Volga and *barbarium*, the Latin for foreign, or from the Greek *rheo* which means "to flow" and refers to its purgative properties. In 1578 it came from Russia to Britain, where it was used as a decorative garden plant and medicinally. Marco Polo wrote that it was exported far and wide from China and in the 13th century it was said to be common in Syria and Persia.

Rhubarb is eaten raw in Alaska by the Eskimos, and in Afghanistan, but it is hardly eaten at all in Spain, Italy or France even though the French imported it in 1724. In 1805 a French gardening book mentioned it as something new and original and the royal gardener under Louis Philippe (1830–48) made another attempt to persuade the French to eat it. At the same time it was eaten in America where the round pouch of unopened flowers was considered a delicacy. The flowers are still eaten in Northern Asia where the variety *Rheum tataricum* is grown especially for its flowers, and the Dutch, Scandinavians and Northern Germans all eat it.

When rhubarb was first introduced the leaves were eaten by mistake. They contain oxalic acid which can be toxic. The fresh, young stalks, however, are juicy, tender and pleasantly tart although old rhubarb is stringy, tough and acidic. Rhubarb mixes well with other fruit and the flavor is enhanced by sugar, ginger, lemon and elderflower. It is almost always used in sweet dishes but Dr. William Kitchiner gave an intriguing recipe for rhubarb soup in his *Cook's Oracle*, published in several editions in the 1820s. He called it Spring Fruit Soup: "Peel and well wash four dozen sticks of Rhubarb; blanch it in water three or four minutes; drain it on a sieve, and put it into a stew-pan, with two Onions sliced, a Carrot, an ounce of lean Ham, and a good bit of Butter; let it stew gently over a slow fire till tender; then put it in two quarts of good Consommé, to which add two or three ounces of Bread-crumbs; boil about fifteen minutes; skim off all the fat; season with salt and Cayenne pepper; pass it through a tamis, and serve up with fried bread."

The recipe here is from *Kezanse Kost (Cadzondse Kost)* by M. A. Aalbregtse, a book of regional food from the area near where Ensor lived, published in 1967. The rhubarb purée can also be used as a filling for a tart. In America, rhubarb pie is traditionally made with a lattice top of pastry, sprinkled with sugar.

RHUBARBER-PAP

"Take sturdy, good red sticks of rhubarb, stripped of outer leaves. Cut into pieces about 2cm long. Wash and put into a pan without water (enough water remains from the washing). Stir occasionally with a wooden spoon. Before it is overcooked, stir well. Now add a lightly beaten egg yolk and sugar and whisk till it becomes frothy. The purée is now finished. Use it warm with cooked potatoes and also as a desert. Recommended also warm as a purgative for school children."

RHUBARB PURÉE

1lb rhubarb, washed, trimmed and cut into 1-in pieces	*1 egg yolk, beaten* *2–4 tbsp soft light brown sugar*

Follow the method in the original recipe.

STILL LIFE WITH MUSHROOMS

Sir William Nicholson (1872–1949)

LONDON (TATE GALLERY)

The mushrooms in this still life by the English artist, Sir William Nicholson (1872–1949), are the largest and best-flavored cultivated mushrooms, *Agaricus bisporus*. Referred to commonly as open, flat or field mushrooms, they are also sometimes found in the wild. Gourmets agree that no cultivated mushroom comes close in flavor to the wild varieties, some 200 species of which are eaten around the world. Of the 80 species consumed by the French, only 20 are found in markets. Finland does rather better with 50 market varieties, but the English and Americans are seldom offered anything other than *A. bisporus*. The oyster mushroom, *Pleurothus ostreatus*, is now appearing in supermarkets in Britain, which is an encouraging sign that Anglo-Saxons are beginning to lose their traditional funghiphobia. But food prejudices die hard and as the *Grete Herball*, published in England in 1526, declared that "tode stooles" were "deedly" and "mussherons" were not, but "they that be not deedly have a grosse gleymy moysture, that is dysobedyent to nature and dygestyon, and be peryllous and dredful to eate & therefor it is good to eschew them," it is not surprising that the British are suspicious of any unfamiliar mushroom.

Some mushrooms, between five to nine species, can be deadly, but only one causes certain death – *Amanita phalloides*, the death cap, which is the cause of 95 per cent of all deaths from mushroom poisoning. The mushroom many connoisseurs consider to have the finest taste, *Amanita caesarea* (the Caesar mushroom), can be confused with the death cap which enabled Agrippina to slip a few of the latter into the dish that her husband, the Emperor Claudius, was about to eat, thus ensuring the succession of her son Nero.

Mushrooms are a useful and delicious food. They have no sugar, hardly any carbohydrate (and what they do comes in the form of indigestible cellulose or fiber) and many vitamins and minerals. They are so rich in protein that they are closer to meat than any other vegetable.

I was once lucky enough to have fresh *Funghi porcini* (picked under a chestnut tree growing near the house in Tuscany where I was a guest) cooked in vine leaves as described by Jane Grigson in *The Mushroom Feast* (1975) and also by Elizabeth David in *Summer Cooking* (1955). But the recipe I use more often than any other is an adaptation, below, of Mrs David's recipe from *French Country Cooking*.

POTAGE AUX CHAMPIGONS A LA BRESSANE

"One thick slice of bread, 1¾ pints stock, 2oz butter, 1lb flat mushrooms, 1 clove chopped garlic, 2 tablespoons chopped parsley, nutmeg or mace, salt and pepper.

Soak the bread in the stock, set aside. Wipe the mushrooms free of grit with a damp cloth or rinse them quickly under running water. Melt the butter in a heavy saucepan. Break the mushrooms into the butter and, when the moisture begins to run, add a small piece of chopped garlic, a tablespoon of chopped parsley, a little salt, freshly milled pepper and grated nutmeg or a pinch of mace (the seasonings are very important). Let the mushrooms cook for several minutes. Squeeze the liquid from the bread and crumble it into the saucepan. Stir with a wooden spoon until it has amalgamated and add the stock. Cook for a further 15 minutes or so. Liquidize until the mixture is the consistency of thin cream broken by all the minuscule particles of the mushrooms."

MUSHROOM SOUP

Serves 8

4 slices fresh white bread	2tbsp chopped parsley
4 cups stock	A pinch of ground mace
¼ cup butter	A pinch of grated nutmeg
1lb large flat mushrooms	Salt and pepper
1 clove garlic, crushed	

Follow the original recipe.

CASSEROLE AND CLOSED MUSSELS

Marcel Broodthaers (1924–1976)

LONDON (TATE GALLERY)

The Belgian artist Marcel Broodthaers has created this witty work of art out of the food universally regarded as his country's national dish. *Mosselen met friten (moules et frites)* – mussels with french fries – are to a Belgian what a hot dog is to an American. Street stalls selling mussels with fries are found all over Belgium but mussels are also often eaten raw, accompanied by a glass of beer. (It was once standard practice to charge a set price for as many mussels as a customer could consume before "coughing.")

Although the mussel, *Mytilus edulis*, is found on both sides of the Atlantic, there was a time when Europeans ate them and Americans did not. The reason why the early settlers avoided them, even though the French, Dutch and English were familiar with them, is that the native Indians warned them off. For some Indians, but not all, mussels were taboo. They thrive on the Atlantic coast of America from the Arctic to Cape Hatteras. Along that strip of coast there were tribes who ate mussels and, in between them, tribes who did not.

On the other, Pacific, coast of America the Indians had worked out that the mussels were poisonous only in the spring when they feed on a plankton, *Gonyaulax* (which contains the poison saxitoxin). When the plankton were numerous enough to cause phosphorescence in the sea the Indians sensibly avoided the mussels.

Mussels were farmed by the Romans at Taranto around 500 BC but the Gauls had been cultivating them even earlier. Charlemagne mentioned them in 800 AD. During the French Revolution it is said that the cook who worked for Citizen Garat, the Minister of Justice, was so outraged when she heard him reading his colleagues a draft of the decree sentencing the King to the guillotine that she tore the paper from his hands and stamped on it. Her tantrum was excused, however, as she then reportedly served them a delicious dish of mussels of her own devising.

Mussels produce an enormous amount of protein and some 10,000lb of meat per acre, even though they take three years to reach a size of 2in long. Healthy mussels snap firmly shut when they are disturbed so discard for cooking any that are already open. A mussel that is heavy may be full of mud, and they must be cleaned carefully to remove barnacles and sand.

The recipe below comes from *The Belgian Cookbook* by Enid Gordon and Midge Shirley.

MOULES A LA BIERE

"Twenty-one mussels (2.25kg), 2 onions, 2 shal-lots, 1 stick celery, 1tsp butter, 33cl (1 bottle) pale ale, 1tsp cornflour, 3 egg yolks, 150g cream, salt and pepper.

Scrape and clean the mussels. Chop the onions, shallots and celery finely. In a deep saucepan, melt the butter, add the mussels and stir. Pour in the beer, add the pepper and very little salt, cover the saucepan and cook the mussels over a medium flame until they have all opened. Remove the mussels, reserving the liquid.

Open the mussels, leaving them in the half shell and layer them in a wide semi-shallow serving dish. Strain the liquid into a smaller saucepan. Mix the cornflour into a paste with a little water and add it to the liquid. Heat this to just under simmering point. Beat the egg yolks and cream and gradually beat in a little hot liquid.

Pour this mixture into the saucepan whisking all the time, until it thickens. It must not boil.

Check the seasoning and pour over the mussels."

MUSSELS WITH BEER

Serves 4

2 quarts fresh mussels	1¼ cups pale ale
2 small onions, chopped	1tsp cornstarch
2 shallots, chopped	3 egg yolks
1 celery stick, chopped	⅔ cup heavy cream
1tsp butter	Salt and pepper

Follow the method in the original recipe.

Feast at the Marriage of Cana *by Paolo Veronese*
(1528–88)
Louvre, Paris.

CHAPTER FOUR

FOOD FOR
CELEBRATION

The ingredients and dishes

associated with festivals and special

occasions

THE KING'S CAKE

Jean-Baptiste Greuze (1725–1805)

PARIS (LOUVRE)

This family group is celebrating the feast of Epiphany on the 6th of January – Twelfth Night – which by the end of the fourth century became identified with the journey of the Magi. It is typical of the artist's rather sentimental genre scenes, one of which, "A Grandfather reading the Bible to his Family," made his name at the Salon of 1755. His popularity with the public and his inflated ego did not endear him to his fellow artists and his attempt at election to the French Academy as a history painter in 1769 was not successful. Following this humiliation he refused to show at the Salon and exhibited privately. His works were in vogue and widely reproduced in engravings throughout the 1770s but the changing fortunes and tastes brought about by the Revolution had disastrous consequences for Greuze and he suffered poverty and neglect during the last decades of his life. He was, however, very popular in Russia and his painting of a "Paralytic tended by his Children" of 1763 hangs today in the Hermitage in Leningrad.

An old Northern European ritual of choosing a king for the day on Twelfth Night by means of a bean hidden in a special cake still exists in some countries. In Denmark, for example, the custom has been translated into an almond in rice pudding. Sadly, Twelfth Night has not survived as a celebration in England. The Long Parliament, during the last days of the Civil War, abolished Christmas and other religious holidays in 1647 but they returned after the Restoration. By the 1880s the elaborate Twelfth Night cakes, games and characters associated with the 6th of January had dwindled to a modest Christmas cake and paper crowns in party favors, the last surviving vestige of the ancient ritual of the "Bean King."

The *Galette des Rois* that survives in France today is an old custom. A flat round cake, its name comes from the word *galet* meaning a weather-worn flat pebble. It is a crown-shaped ring of puff pastry filled with almond paste (in Paris, Lyon and north of the Loire); elsewhere it can be a sweet brioche, studded with candied fruit – all with a bean baked inside. Gold or silver paper crowns are usually provided free with bakers' cakes.

The scene depicted in the painting still takes place all over France. A child, usually the youngest member of the assembly, hides and, as the cake is cut, is asked by an adult, "For whom is this piece?" The person who gets the piece with the bean is crowned king or

The following recipe is taken from *Petits Propos Culinaires 27* by James Bauman (Prospect Books) 1987.

GALETTE DES ROIS

"250g (1¾ cups) flour; 190g (7oz) butter (unsalted); 5g (1tsp) salt; 7g (2tsp) sugar; ¾dl (⅓ cup) water; an egg yolk blended with 2tsp water, to glaze the galette. Make a well in the flour, put the slightly softened butter into it. Dissolve the salt and sugar in the water, pour in to the well. With your fingers (or a fork) roughly mix the butter and water, gradually incorporating the flour until you have a rather firm dough. Do not knead. Gather it into a ball, flour lightly, wrap and let rest for ¾ hour in a cool place.

On a floured surface, roll out the dough into a rectangle about 60 × 22cm (24 × 8in). Fold in thirds and let rest 10 minutes. Repeat this operation twice, always rolling and folding in the opposite direction. After the third 'turn' fold the corners up over the dough to form a round pad. Roll out to a disc 1.5–2cm (about ¾in) thick. With the back of a knife notch the rim at intervals, evening out the circle if necessary. With the point of the knife, make a slit in the edge, insert a bean and reseal. If you will want to know where it is later insert it underneath the dough and mark the spot. Place on an egg glaze, taking care not to let it drip over the edge. Score with grill work or any other design, with the tines of a fork (or the point of a knife). Prick through in several places.

Bake in a moderately hot preheated oven (450°F) for 30–35 minutes. (For a shinier, sweeter glaze, dust with powdered sugar a few minutes before removing.) Cool on a rack. The galette is always served warm; if need be, reheat it to that point."

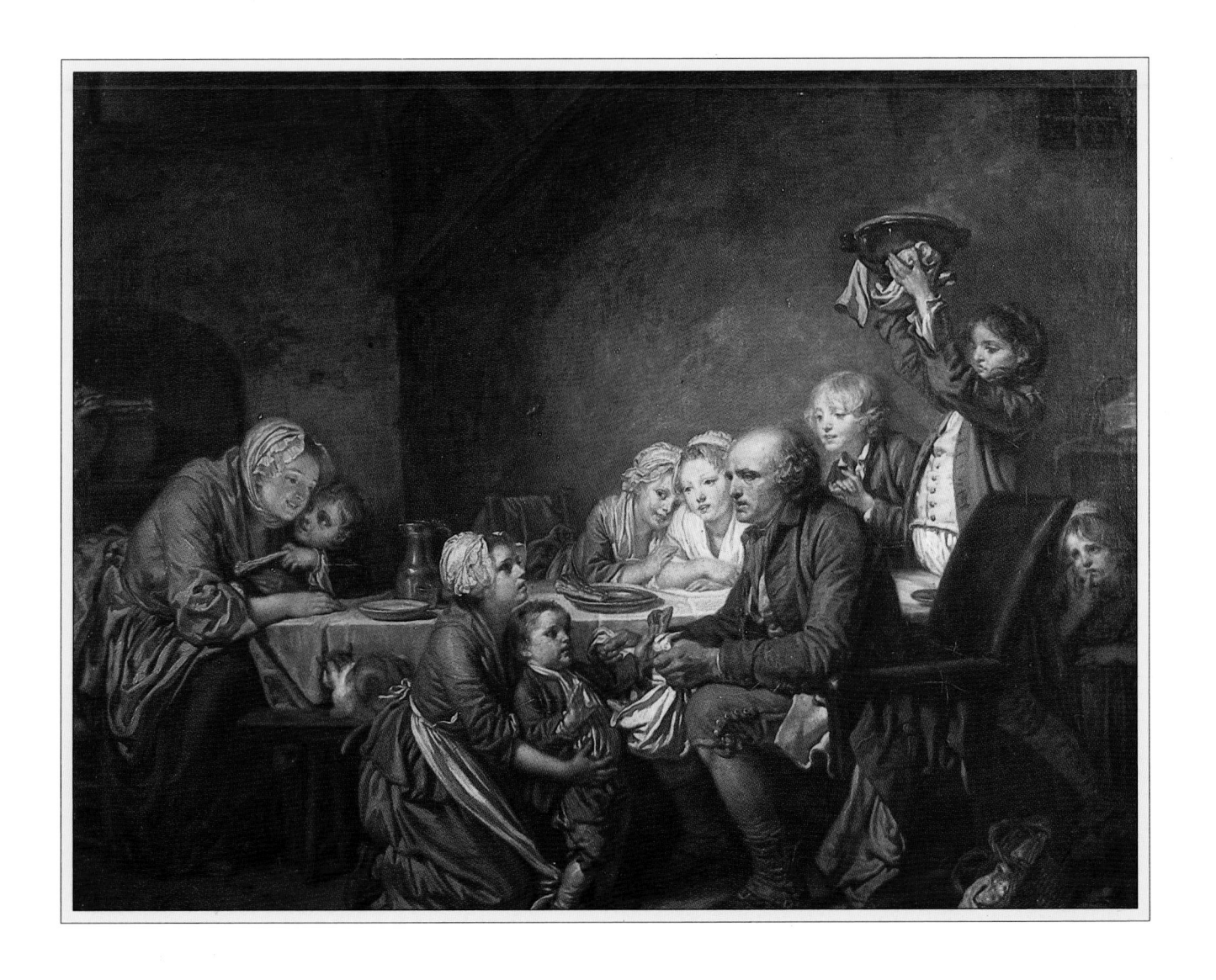

DINNER FOR THRESHERS

Grant Wood (1892–1942)

SAN FRANCISCO (FINE ART MUSEUM)

The American artist Grant Wood (1892–1942) from the Mid western state of Iowa, is best known for his portrait of a starkly posed farmer-preacher and his daughter, modeled by his sister Nan, and his dentist B. H. McKeeby. Entitled "American Gothic," the painting was a sensation in 1930 and has become an icon of Americana as familiar in the United States, and as often parodied, as the Mona Lisa. Employed by the Army to paint camouflage during the First World War, Wood taught art in high school after he left the Army and then spent a year in Paris at the Académie Julien in 1923. When he returned to Cedar Rapids, Iowa, his first patron, a local mortician, gave him a studio and a place to live. In 1927 he was commissioned to design the stained glass windows for the American Legion building and went to Munich to have them executed. The Legionnaires rejected the windows and Wood retaliated with a painting called "The Daughters of Revolution" that was a satirical comment on the establishment. After the success of "American Gothic" his paintings were in demand and in 1934 he was made a professor of fine arts at the University of Iowa in Iowa City, where he remained until he died.

The threshers in this painting are probably harvesting corn. Iowa has more top quality farming land than any other state (almost 90 per cent of its total area) and half of it is used to grown corn – Iowa is the largest producer in the United States.

The food of the American Midwest is still heavily influenced by the large number of immigrants from Northern Europe who went there in the 19th century. In the 1830s, 30 per cent of all the new arrivals were from Germany, many of them political refugees. The population of the Midwest was also swelled with Scandinavians. Most of the Swedish colonies, for example, were in Washington, Nebraska, Illinois, Minnesota and Iowa and large numbers of them be-came farmers.

Many of the food traditions the settlers brought with them have become so completely absorbed into the American diet that no-one thinks of them as being anything other than typically American. Frankfurters, hamburgers, doughnuts and pretzels came with the Germans; pancakes and *koekje* (cookie), and coleslaw – from *cool* (cabbage) and *sla* (salad) – with the Dutch.

Clementine Paddleford, the author of *How America Eats*, published in 1960, explained in her foreword that she started traveling around America as roving Food Editor for *This Week* magazine in 1948. In 12 years she covered over 800,000 miles. In Iowa she met Edith Davison, a home economics graduate from Iowa State College who was the catering manager for the Des Moines Iowa Women's Club. She grew up on a farm in Mills County, and this recipe for Apple Relish was one of her mother's. It is typical of the pickles and relishes common in any area populated by northern Europeans.

APPLE RELISH

"1 lb large red apples, 2 dill pickles, 1 medium onion, ½ cup sugar, ¼ cup vinegar. Core apples but do not peel; grind together with pickles and onion. Add sugar and vinegar. Serve well chilled with pork or turkey. Yield: 1 pint relish."

Makes 4 jars

1lb red skinned apples	*½ cup sugar*
2 large dill pickles	*¼ cup vinegar*
1 small onion	

Quarter and core the apples, but do not peel them. Coarsely grate the apples and pickles and onion (in a food processor, if preferred). Add the sugar and vinegar, and transfer to sterilized jars. Serve well chilled with pork or turkey. It keeps well in the fridge.

MAKING THE EMPIRE CHRISTMAS PUDDING

F. C. Harrison 20th century

LONDON (PUBLIC RECORDS OFFICE)

Christmas pudding, like that other staple of the festive season, the mince pie, has a long history. Both contain dried fruit and peel which were imported along with spices from Southern Europe – raisins of Corinth, or prunes, dried figs and dates. The rich used them to liven up Lenten fare but the poor could only afford them as a special treat in pottages and pies during the 12 days of Christmas. An importer who had not sold his dried fruit before Easter when fresh fruit came into season was in trouble.

The pudding as we know it began life as "Stewed Broth" first mentioned in the 15th century. "Stewet beef to pottage" was gobbets of beef boiled in water and wine with minced onions and fine herbs, thickened with bread, seasoned with powdered cloves, cinnamon and mace, colored red with saunders (sandalwood) and studded with currants.

The Elizabethans stewed broth with veal, mutton or cock and added dried plums (prunes). The 17th-century cookery writer, Gervase Markham, recommends it as a special dish for the first course on All Saints Day, Christmas Day and New Year and in 1673 another writer, William Rabisha, mentions it as being specifically for Christmas as Christmas Broth or pottage or Plum Pottage or porridge. Eighteenth-century plum puddings for Christmas rarely had any alcohol but Plum Porridge was laced with wine or sack, made well before the season began and then stored in earthenware pots. The meat content had largely disappeared by the 19th century but the Scottish writer, Meg Dogs, gives one of the last Plum Porridge recipes with meat in it in 1826.

The most important dish on the medieval Christmas table was brawn made originally from wild boar and later from tame boars or pigs, which was cooked so tender "that a man may thrust a bruised rush or straw clean through the fat" wrote the Elizabethan, William Harrison. As late as the 19th century Hannah Glasse explained in her celebrated cookbook, *The Art of Cookery Made Plain and Easy*, how to distinguish brawn of real boar from that of barrow-hog or sow – by the thickness of the rind. In the same century Elizabeth Raffald gave a recipe for mock brawn made from the belly and head of a young pig and interlarded with oxfeet.

This recipe was created by M. Henri Cédard, the Maître Chef to King George V, and included in Elizabeth Craig's book, *Court Favourites*, 1953.

EMPIRE CHRISTMAS PUDDING

"5lb Australian currants, 5lb Australian sultanas, 5lb South African stoned raisins, 1½lb minced Canadian apples, 5lb United Kingdom breadcrumbs, 5lb New Zealand beef suet, 2lb South African cut candied peel, 2½lb United Kingdom flour, 2½lb West Indies Demerara sugar, 20 eggs (Irish Free State), 2oz Ceylon ground cinnamon, 1½oz Zanzibar ground cloves, 1½oz ground nutmegs (Straits Settlements), 1tsp Indian pudding spice, ¼ pint Cyprus brandy, ½ pint Jamaica rum, 2 quarts Old English Beer.

Place all the dry ingredients in a basin. Mix well and add the eggs, stirring well. Add the liquid and stir to mix thoroughly. Press into greased pudding basins. Steam for six hours and when required steam again for 6 hours."

Makes three 2-lb puddings

2⅔ cups currants	4 eggs
2⅔ cups golden raisins	2tbsp ground cinnamon
2⅔ cups raisins	1tbsp ground cloves
6oz cooking apples	1tbsp grated nutmeg
8 cups fresh bread crumbs	¼tsp mixed spice
2 cups beef suet	2tbsp brandy
¾ cup candied peel	¼ cup rum
2 cups all-purpose flour	1½ cups light ale
Heaped 1 cup brown sugar	

Mix all the ingredients thoroughly together. Divide between three heatproof bowls, well greased. Cover and steam for 6 hours. Cool and store. Steam again for 6 hours on day it is to be served. The longer the cooking, the darker the pudding will be.

ROYAL TEA PARTY AT WINDSOR

Sir James Gunn (1893–1964)

LONDON (NATIONAL PORTRAIT GALLERY)

The young Princess Elizabeth, now Queen Elizabeth II, is shown here having tea with her family at Windsor Castle – an afternoon ritual that has been a British national institution since the middle of the last century. By the 1820s, the fashionable had begun to dine later and later in the evening. The wife of the 7th Duke of Bedford is credited with arranging the first tea parties. Unable to cope with hunger pangs, she is said to have started the custom by inviting a few selected friends to her room for tea, bread and butter to keep them going until the dinner hour.

In 1664, a present of 2lb 2oz of tea was given to King Charles II by the East India Company, which began importing tea directly from China in 1689. Tea soon became the national drink, consumed at regular intervals, by all classes of society, even though in the 18th century, for example, a pound of the cheapest tea cost a third of a skilled worker's weekly wage. Today, the British still drink a great deal of tea – almost half of that drunk in the world.

One of Britain's most prestigious industries, the manufacture of high-quality ceramics, was a result of the British passion for tea. Teapots and cups were originally imported from China with the tea chests, but a desire to reproduce Chinese tea wares was directly responsible for the rise of the Staffordshire potteries.

The making of true porcelain was a secret closely guarded by the Chinese, and potters in the West were anxious to discover it. A French factory at St. Cloud had managed to make a substitute called soft-paste before the end of the 17th century but it was not until 1713 that hard-paste porcelain from Meissen was triumphantly introduced at the Leipzig fair. Teapots and eventually complete tea sets formed the major part of the factory's output.

By 1745 two Frenchmen, Gouyn and Sprimont, originally silversmiths, were making St. Cloud soft-paste at a factory in Chelsea. Potteries in Bow, Derby and Worcester soon followed suit and it was during this period that English tea wares reached their height of beauty and elegance: these pieces are now valuable collectors' items.

The recipe here dates from 1839 and comes from *Court Favourites – Recipes from Royal Kitchens* by Elizabeth Craig, published in 1953 (the year of Queen Elizabeth II's coronation). Many of the recipes come either from a scrapbook originally owned by Princess Charlotte, daughter of George IV and Caroline of Brunswick, and given to Queen Victoria when she was a young girl or from another scrap book of recipes also owned by a member of the Royal Family. This cake was sent every year from Cumberland to Queen Victoria on her birthday.

CUMBERLAND GINGER SHORTCAKE

"Half-a-pound sifted flour, pinch of salt, ½tsp bicarbonate of soda, ½tsp cream of tartar, powdered ginger to taste, ¼lb brown sugar, ¼lb butter. Mix all dry ingredients together. Rub in butter. Stir well, then put into a well-buttered tin, pressing down firmly with the back of a wooden spoon. The cake should be level and only half an inch deep. No moistening required. Bake in a moderate oven for about half an hour."

Makes 8 wedges

2 cups all-purpose flour	Heaped ½ cup dark
A pinch of salt	brown sugar
½tsp baking soda	½ cup butter
½tsp cream of tartar	A well-buttered 9-in shallow
1tbsp ground ginger	pie plate

Sift the flour, salt, baking soda, cream of tartar and ginger into a bowl. Add the sugar and butter and rub together – the warmth from your hands helps to bind the ingredients. Press firmly into the pie plate using a potato masher to level surface. Prick all over. Bake at 350°F for 30–35 minutes. Cool on a wire rack.

PRIVATE VIEW
Beryl Cook
(PRIVATE COLLECTION)

The buxom waitress in this painting is bearing her tray of canapés through the hectic throng at an art gallery at an event obviously well known to the artist. The opening of a new exhibition, attended by the painter's critics, patrons and friends, is now called a "private view" and has replaced the *vernissage* (varnishing day) when an artist would invite friends around to see his newly completed but as yet unvarnished works. In this painting, the crowd are enjoying a form of hospitality known as a "drinks party" – formerly called a "cocktail party." The American writer Brooks Atkinson scathingly remarked in 1951 that the cocktail party "has the form of friendship without the warmth and devotion. It is a device either for getting rid of social obligations hurriedly *en masse*, or for making overtures toward more serious social relationships, as in the etiquette of whoring."

The Savoy Cocktail Book, first published in 1930 and still in print, mentions in a "Historical Note" that the first printed reference to the cocktail was in an American periodical, *The Balance* (May 13, 1806), which defined it thus: "*Cock tail*, then, is a stimulating liquor, composed of *spirits* of any kind, *sugar*, *water* and *bitters* – it is vulgarly called *bittered sling* and is supposed to be an excellent electioneering potion."

In the classic cookbook of Constance Spry and Rosemary Hume, *The Constance Spry Cookery Book*, published in 1956, the authors introduce the book by saying that "Perhaps a cookery book should start in a less frivolous fashion than with a chapter headed The Cocktail Party." They quote from an article Rebecca West wrote for the *New Yorker* in 1953 about William Martin Marshall who was tried for espionage. Rebecca West is explaining that Marshall's parents thought he had been corrupted in Russia and introduced to a life to which he was not accustomed. "There were continual parties. Cocktail parties. The sharp sound of the words, flung out after a preparatory pause, recalled that there was an age not so long ago when a cocktail was considered an immoral drink, as different from sherry as concubinage is from

marriage, and a cocktail party meant an assembly of people who had abandoned normal restraints.'

Anyone who has ever consumed alcohol on an empty stomach will deplore the barbaric insensitivity of serving strong drink without food. Elsie de Wolfe (Lady Mendl), an influential socialite and interior decorator, wrote *Recipes for Successful Dining* in 1934. Her list of "Suggestions for Tea-Cocktail Parties" is a long one. Hot small sausages are still *de rigueur* and many of the recipes would tempt a modern hostess including hot buttered soda biscuits, baby fish cakes, toasted cheese biscuits, cold stuffed eggs (the yolks mixed with anchovy paste and butter, with a dash of cayenne), olives wrapped in bacon (roasted almonds inserted in pitted olives, wrapped in bacon secured with a toothpick and broiled), and Indian sardine squares (split boneless sardines filled with Indian mango chutney, placed on small lettuce leaves and then on pieces of toast).

The recipe for these canapés, called Marbury Rolls, came from Miss Elizabeth Marbury of New York.

MARBURY ROLLS

"Take very fresh sandwich bread. Cut in very thin slices and butter. Fry bacon and chop very fine. Then put a little roll of the bacon in the middle of each slice, sprinkle with grated Parmesan cheese, and finely chopped parsley. Also sprinkle with a generous quantity of paprika and a very small dash of cayenne pepper. Roll like a cigarette and hold together with a wooden toothpick. Put on a tin platter and grill in the oven, until nicely browned, and serve hot."

Makes 12 rolls. Cut in half to make 24 rolls to serve as cocktail snacks.

12 thin slices white bread (crusts removed and lightly buttered)	*2tbsp chopped parsley*
	½tsp ground paprika
7 slices of bacon	*A pinch of cayenne pepper*
2tbsp grated Parmesan	*Wooden toothpicks*

Follow the original method.

Huaxtec Civilization *by Diego Rivera, 18th century*
National Museum of Mexico.

CHAPTER FIVE

FOOD
FROM THE
NEW WORLD

The wonderful diversity
of ingredients that were
introduced following the
discovery of the Americas

KITCHEN MAID WITH POULTRY

Bernardo Strozzi (1581–1644)

GENOA (PALAZZO ROSSO)

Bernardo Strozzi's biography reads like the plot of a racy adventure story. Born in Genoa in 1581, he became a Capuchin friar by the age of 17. In 1610, when he was 29, he was allowed to leave the monastery to support his widowed mother, which he did by pursuing a successful career as a painter. After she died in 1630 he began a long struggle with the church authorities who wanted him to return to his order. He had no wish to return to the confines of a cloister, and kidnappings and disguises were employed to effect his escape to the safety of Venice in 1631.

As a painter, his work was greatly influenced by Peter Paul Rubens and possibly also by Van Dyck who were both in Genoa in the early 1600s. Most of Strozzi's paintings are of gentle religious subjects and "genre" scenes such as this one of a kitchen maid plucking poultry.

She is presumably preparing the birds for a grand occasion as both swan and turkey were very much a luxury. When Archbishop Cranmer attempted to temper the excesses of the clergy in England he listed the great fowls, which included crane, swan and turkey, and ruled that only one of each could be included in a single dish.

The turkey was one import from the New World that was immediately popular – cooks already knew what to do with big birds. Both the potato and the tomato took very much longer to catch on.

By the end of the 16th century one German cookery book gave 20 different ways of serving turkey. In France in the 18th century French sympathizers with the American Revolution ate it as a symbol of solidarity, and Benjamin Franklin thought so highly of it that he wrote to his daughter in 1784 complaining that the eagle, which he called "a bird of bad moral character," had been chosen to represent America rather than the turkey – a "much more respectable bird, and withal a true native original of America."

The two groups of English settlers in America – Captain John Smith in Jamestown, Virginia, and the Pilgrims who landed in New England – were both given turkeys by the Indians. The Pilgrim Fathers ate turkeys at the first Thanksgiving dinner in 1621: they were already familiar birds as the Spanish had brought them to Europe earlier, in 1523 or 1524.

The following recipe comes from *La Nuovissima Cucina Economica* (see page 40).

ALE ALLA CHIOZOTTA

"Prepare the turkey wings but do not remove the bones. Make a lukewarm marinade out of a piece of butter, a little flour, half a glass vinegar, a little water or broth, salt and pepper, half a clove of garlic and two cloves, a slice of onion, a piece of carrot, a little bay, parsley stalks, the zest of an orange and a little basil. Leave the turkey in the marinade for four hours. Dry the pieces with a clean cloth. Moisten in beaten egg white. Dip in flour, fry in lard and serve garnished with fried parsley."

TURKEY WINGS, CHIOGGIA-STYLE

Serves 6

2¼lb of turkey wings

Marinade

1tbsp butter	1 small carrot, coarsely grated
1tbsp flour	Parsley stalks
⅓ cup wine vinegar	1 small bay leaf
⅔ cup water or stock	The finely grated rind of
Salt and pepper	1 orange
1 clove garlic, crushed	A few fresh basil leaves,
2 pinches of ground cloves	chopped
1 small onion, finely sliced	

To finish

1 egg white	½ cup shortening or dripping
2tbsp flour	

Put the turkey wings in a shallow dish. Melt the butter, add the flour and blend in the vinegar and water. Bring to a boil to thicken, simmer for a minute. Season with salt and pepper, and add the remaining marinade ingredients. Pour over the turkey wings and leave for 4 hours, turning the wings over once.

Drain the wings, dry each one, brush with beaten egg white and roll in flour to coat. Fry gently in hot shortening for about 10 minutes until browned all over. Drain.

KITCHEN SCENE, 1618

Diego Velazquez (1599–1660)

LONDON (NATIONAL GALLERY)

Diego Velazquez, born in Seville in 1599, was one of the greatest Spanish painters of all time, and certainly the most important Spanish artist of the 17th century. His work was influenced by 16th-century Venetian painting and the dramatic use of light and dark, called "tenebrism," associated with Caravaggio (1573–1610). His early paintings were religious and genre subjects, and he was known for his *bodegones*, or kitchen scenes, with still lifes incorporated in them. This painting is a *bodegon* with a religious scene tucked into the background.

Velazquez was called to Madrid in 1623 by the First Minister, Count Olivares, who also came from Seville. Velazquez had been there the previous year seeking royal patronage from the recently crowned King Philip IV. The portrait he executed of the King was a success and as a result he was appointed court painter, with the promise that he would be the only painter to portray the monarch.

His father-in-law and early teacher, the less talented Francisco Pacheco, wrote, "He has a workshop in his gallery and His Majesty has a key to it and a chair in order to watch him painting at leisure, nearly every day."

The King sent him to Venice in 1631 to buy paintings from Titian, Tintoretto and Veronese, and also to Modena, Bologna, and Rome, where he met fellow artists Poussin and Bernini. His last royal commission was to accompany the King and court in the spring of 1660 to the French border, where he was in charge of the decoration of the Spanish pavilion for the marriage of the Infanta Maria Theresa to Louis XIV. Not long after his return to Madrid he became ill, and he died on 6th August 1660.

The most interesting item of food in this painting is the red chili peppers beside the mortar and pestle. It was Christopher Columbus who first described chilies as peppers. The Arawaks in the West Indies gave him hot spicy food and, as he thought he was in India, he assumed that the source of the hotness was pepper (*Piper nigrum*) (which comes from India). He was wrong. It came from the fruit of *Capsicum frutescens*, known as *aji* (the Arawak word) or chili (the Aztec word). In English *Capsicum annuum* are called sweet peppers or bell peppers, and *Capsicum frutescens*, chili peppers.

Chilies have been found in pre-historic Inca sites in Peru and were used extensively by the Aztecs before the arrival of the Spanish. Mexicans use more chilies than any other nation, over half of the 200 or so types.

No other New World food achieved the global acceptance given to the chili. Poor people all over the world use them, they make almost any food more interesting and are a valuable source of vitamin C.

This recipe is adapted from *Adventures in Taste: The Wines & Folk Food of Spain* by D. E. Pohren, published by the Society of Spanish Studies in Seville in 1972.

PATITAS EN MOJO

"1 lb small new potatoes, dry hot red pepper to taste, 2tbsp vinegar, 1tsp paprika, 2tbsp olive oil, 2 cloves garlic, peeled, ½tsp cumin seeds, salt to taste. Boil the potatoes in their skins. Blend the other ingredients in a mortar or blender, adding the oil a little at a time and then the vinegar. If the sauce is too thick, add a little water. Serve the potatoes hot, mixed with the sauce."

POTATOES IN CHILI SAUCE

Serves 4

1lb small new potatoes	Salt and pepper
A pinch of hot chili powder	2 cloves garlic, crushed
1tsp ground paprika	2tbsp olive oil
½tsp cumin seeds	2tbsp vinegar

Scrub the potatoes thoroughly, boil in their skins until tender. Drain well. Meanwhile, combine the remaining ingredients in a mortar and pestle or blender until smooth.

Return potatoes to pan, add sauce and heat gently for a minute or two. Serve at once.

MOOR GRATING CHOCOLATE

Anon, Spanish (c. 1750–70)

RALEIGH (NORTH CAROLINA MUSEUM OF ART)

The man in the painting is preparing the fruit of the cacao tree, *Theobroma cacao* (*theobroma* means "food of the gods"). The flower of the tree, indigenous to the American tropics, produces an oval pod filled with a white, sweet, viscous material which encloses some 30 to 40 seeds. (One Indian tribe in the Orinoco region of Venezuela sucked the pulp and threw away the seeds.) The pods are gathered as they ripen and are then split and allowed to dry out for 24 hours.

Chocolate was a favorite food of the Aztecs and the bitter chocolate drink given by them to the Spaniards was found to be both refreshing and stimulating, thanks to the presence of two alkaloids – theobromine and caffeine. It has recently been discovered that chocolate contains another chemical, phenylethylmine, which is related to a natural substance similar to amphetamines and is capable of producing exhilarating peaks of excitement and slumps of deepest gloom similar to those often experienced by persons in love.

When chocolate arrived in Europe from the New World it was made into a drink, as it had been in America, and its popularity came not just from its novelty (and expense), but also from its reputation as a restorative. Samuel Pepys wrote in his diary for 24th April, 1661 (the day after the coronation of Charles II, which he had obviously celebrated merrily), "Waked in the morning with my head in a sad taking through last night's drink, which I am very sorry for. So rose and went out with Mr. Creed to drink our morning draught, which he did give me in chocolate to settle my stomach."

Chocolate is highly nutritious, the bean itself contains 49 per cent oil, 18 per cent protein, 10 per cent starch and 7 per cent other carbohydrates. Modern milk chocolate typically contains 520 calories per 100g/3½oz and contains 57 per cent carbohydrate and 32 per cent fat. It is also particularly rich in potassium, calcium and magnesium with significant amounts of vitamins A, B1, B2 and B3.

Chocolate is the only New World foodstuff that has romantic associations. Even though the tomato was once called a "love apple" you would hardly give the beloved a gift of one, but chocolates are universally regarded as a token of esteem, if not always of desire.

This recipe is adapted from *Adventures in Taste: The Wines & Folk Food of Spain* by D. E. Pohren, published by the Society of Spanish Studies in Seville in 1972.

PERDIZ CON CHOCOLATE

"Two large partridge; ½ cup vinegar; 4 unpeeled cloves garlic; ½ cup white wine; 4 black peppercorns; 1 bay leaf, crumbled; salt to taste; water to cover; 2 ounces cooking chocolate; 16 small onions; 4 slices French bread, fried in olive oil until brown. Marinate the birds with the vinegar, garlic, wine, peppercorns, bay leaf, salt and enough water to cover for several hours or overnight. Sauté the drained birds in olive oil until golden, add the marinade and simmer covered over a low heat for 1½–2 hours until they are tender. Remove the birds and reduce the sauce by rapid boiling until it is thick enough to coat a spoon. Add the onions to the sauce and cook quickly for about 15 minutes, remove the onions and add the chocolate, stirring until it is completely dissolved. Put the birds and onions back into the sauce and cook just long enough to heat them through. Place on a hot serving dish the fried bread, then the partridges and pour the sauce over it and serve hot. Wild pigeon or quail can be cooked in the same way."

PARTRIDGE WITH CHOCOLATE

Serves 4

2 large partridge (or 4 wood pigeon or quail)	1 bay leaf, crumbled
½ cup vinegar	Salt and pepper
4 cloves garlic, unpeeled but bruised	1¼ cups water
½ cup white wine	2 squares cooking chocolate
4 black peppercorns	16 small pearl onions
	4 thick slices French bread
	Olive oil for shallow frying

Clean the birds thoroughly, and then follow the original recipe.

LAST SUPPER

Anon, 17th century

CUZCO (CUZCO CATHEDRAL)

The Last Supper this unknown Peruvian artist chose as his subject is one that Christian artists have depicted over many centuries. What happened at the Jewish Passover meal celebrated by Christ and his 12 apostles was later described by four of the people present. This event in the life of Christ is told in all four gospels of the New Testament, by Matthew, Mark, Luke and John.

The earlier representations of the Last Supper as the first communion of the apostles had evolved by the time it was executed in mosaic by Byzantine artists of the sixth century. At this time the participants are shown reclining around a D-shaped table, with Christ at one end, propped up on one elbow with the right arm free as was the custom at Passover.

This painting from Cuzco Cathedral was painted when the Spanish and the Church were firmly established in Peru and we can assume that the meal on the table is one that a contemporary Peruvian peasant would recognize. When the Spaniard, Francisco Pizarro, traveled to Peru in 1530 with his three brothers and 200 adventure seekers, the Inca Empire was highly organized, covering vast territory north of the Andes with more than 7 million people. Fortunately for the Spanish, it was under attack from within. A civil war was raging when they arrived and it was through treachery that Pizarro was able to seize the Inca ruler Atahualpa. He was held to ransom and callously strangled when it was paid. Within three years the Spanish were in control but pockets of Inca resistance held out for another 30 years before the Incas were finally vanquished.

One of the most important foods the Spanish found in South America was the potato, first encountered by a European early in 1537. Juan de Castellanos described "truffles" (potatoes), maize and beans in his account of an expedition with Gonzalo Jimenez de Quesada. They were said to be "of good flavor, a gift very acceptable to Indians and a dainty dish even for Spaniards."

The following recipe is taken from *The Book of LatinAmerican Cookery* by Elizabeth Lambert Ortiz.

CARAPULCRA

"Two fresh potatoes (or 2 freeze-dried potatoes), a 2½lb chicken, cut into serving pieces, 1lb loin of pork, cut into ¾in cubes, ¾pt chicken stock, about 4tbsp lard or vegetable oil, 1 large onion, finely chopped, 4 cloves garlic, minced, ½tsp Spanish (hot) paprika or cayenne, ⅛tsp ground cumin, salt, freshly ground pepper, 2oz roasted peanuts, finely ground, 6 small potatoes, freshly cooked, 3 hardboiled eggs, sliced, 20 medium-sized stoned black or green olives.

Put the dried potatoes on to soak in warm water to cover for about 2 hours. Drain them, chop coarsely and set aside.

Put the chicken and pork pieces into a saucepan and add enough chicken stock to cover. Cover and simmer until tender. Drain and set the stock aside. Bone the chicken and cut the meat into cubes about the same size as the pork. Set aside with a little stock to moisten the meats.

Rinse out and dry the saucepan or use a flameproof casserole, and heat the lard or oil in it. Add the onion, garlic, hot paprika or cayenne and cumin, and sauté until the onion is soft. Add the potato and about ½pt of the reserved stock, cover, and simmer gently until the potato has disintegrated, thickening the mixture, about 1 hour. Season to taste with salt and pepper and stir in the ground peanuts. Cook for a minute or two, then add the chicken and pork pieces. The sauce should be thick, but add a little more stock if necessary. Simmer just long enough to heat through and blend the flavours.

Arrange the chicken and pork mixture on a heated serving platter and garnish it with the fresh, hot potatoes, the hardboiled egg slices, and olives."

THE CUP OF CHOCOLATE

François Boucher (1703–70)

PARIS (LOUVRE)

François Boucher was the protégé and friend of Madame de Pompadour, the stylish mistress of King Louis XV. Some of his most beautiful paintings are exquisite portraits of his patron and all his work embodies perfectly the graceful Rococo style. When his subjects were not slightly risqué mythological scenes, he painted the aristocracy taking their fashionable pleasures. At the time this delicious domestic scene was executed, chocolate drinking was a luxury, beyond the means of anyone not in the upper strata of society.

Chocolate was discovered in the 16th century in Mexico by the Spanish conquistadors. According to an eye-witness account by Bernal Diaz who traveled in Mexico with Cortez, Montezuma drank chocolate from solid gold cups. The Aztec chief, warriors, and nobles of the court made a drink of pure cacao, which was kept in gold jars. It was well-beaten and flavored with vanilla, wild honey, maguey (century plant), and occasionally chilies. The poorer population drank cacao mixed with corn flour and seasoned with hot chili pepper.

The Spanish took to chocolate and opened up *chocolaterias*, rather like tea rooms, where chocolate was prepared and drunk throughout the West Indies. The practice spread to Spain where the chocolate was flavored with cinnamon, nutmeg, pepper and ginger and then to Italy in 1600. In France the first person on record as using chocolate was the older brother of Cardinal Richelieu who took it for "splenic vapors," sometime before 1642. When Maria Theresa, the daughter of Philip IV of Spain, went to France to marry Louis XIV she traveled with a maid whose job it was to prepare drinking chocolate, for which the future queen had a passion. What royalty did, the fashionable copied.

Chocolate was not adopted in England until the middle of the 17th century. Its popularity in France became more widespread in the 18th century with the establishment of the royal chocolate factory in 1776. Pope Pius V had conveniently decreed that it did not break the Lenten fasting rules.

Chocolate was originally prepared with carved wooden chocolate mills which are still widely available in Mexico and must be very like the ones called for in Menon's recipe for chocolate from *The Professed Cook*, the English translation of *Les Soupers de la Cour* which was published in 1755 in France and, slightly later, in 1767, in England.

CHOCOLATE

"Simmer the chocolate on a slow fire, in the proportion of two ounces to each Cup; Stir it about a good deal with a Chocolate-mill, and when it is properly dissolved and thickened, add a yolk of an Egg, beat up, to the proportion of four Cups, or the Whites equally beat up, and the first froth thrown away; mix it first with a little of the chocolate, which add to the rest, and mill it very well to incorporate together; This will make it of a proper consistence and of a better froth. It is best to be made a day or two before using. If you keep ready made at any time, boil it a moment every other day; sweeten it according to taste."

BEATEN CHOCOLATE

Makes 2 large or 4 small cups

8 squares semi-sweet chocolate	2 egg whites
1 egg yolk	Superfine sugar

Put the chocolate in a bowl over very hot water. Heat gently to melt, beat until smooth and then beat in the egg yolk. Beat the whites with clean beaters until stiff. Add a little of the hot chocolate to the egg whites, then mix the egg white mixture into the rest of the chocolate until well blended. Best made one or two days before using; sweeten to taste before serving.

STILL LIFE WITH WATERMELONS

Raphaelle Peale (1774–1825)

WASHINGTON (NATIONAL GALLERY OF ART)

Raphaelle Peale is regarded as the most accomplished of a family of artists. His father, Charles Wilson, and his uncle, James, were both painters. Raphaelle, born in 1774, was one of 17 children; his father had three wives, and died at the age of 86 while courting his intended fourth. Raphaelle's brothers, Rembrandt, Rubens and Titian, were also painters, but no works by his sisters, Angelica Kauffmann, Rosalba Carriera and Sophonisba (if they did paint), have survived. Raphaelle painted these melons in 1813.

Watermelon is probably native to Africa although it was naturalized in the Middle East and Russia before recorded history. There is a word for it in Sanskrit which dates from the beginning of the first millennium BC. The Moors introduced it to Southern Europe after the fall of the Roman Empire, the Chinese cultivated it in the 10th century AD, and Negro slaves brought watermelon, okra and black-eyed pea seeds from Africa to the New World, where all three are still firmly associated with the American South.

A member of the cucumber family, *Citrullus vulgaris*, watermelon is 91 per cent water and 8 per cent carbohydrate, low in calories and one of the most refreshing of summer fruits. Farm workers in New Jersey in 1770 were described as eating watermelons from the fields "at any time of day as laborers in England would drink ale or small beer."

Mark Twain, who created two of the most enduring characters in American fiction, Tom Sawyer, whose adventures were published in 1876, and Huckleberry Finn (published in 1885), called watermelon "chief of the world's luxuries" and wrote "when one has tasted it, he knows what angels eat."

Marion Cabell Tyree gives several recipes for Watermelon Rind Pickle in *Housekeeping in Old Virginia*, published in Louisville, Kentucky, in 1879. "Trim the rinds nicely, being careful to cut off the hard coating with the outer green," she wrote. The rind is then gently boiled for half an hour and left to drain overnight. For 10lb of rind, a quart of vinegar, 3lb of brown sugar, an ounce of cinnamon and mace, and 3 teaspoonfuls of turmeric, is boiled with the beaten white of an egg. When the liquid is clear, the rind is boiled in it for 20 minutes with the peel of two fresh lemons which, she says, "will give a nice flavor, though not at all necessary."

Americans often eat watermelon with salt, as a pinch of it enhances the sweetness of some fruit. A lightly salted watermelon ice between courses on a hot summer's day would provide an intriguing pause in the meal.

A food processor eliminates the need for egg white in a water ice, and makes preparing the fruit the work of seconds. Process the mixture when it is partly frozen, whip it to a froth and put it back in the freezer. Alternatively, use a sorbetier.

Marion Cabell Tyree describes watermelon ice (below) as "beautiful and delicious:"

WATERMELON ICE

"Select a ripe and very red melon. Scrape some of the pulp and use all the water. A few of the seeds interspersed will add greatly to the appearance. Sweeten to the taste and freeze as you would any other ice. If you wish it very light, add the whites of three eggs, thoroughly whipped, to one gallon of the icing just as it begins to congeal. Beat frequently and very hard with a large iron spoon."

Serves 6–8

1 ripe watermelon	2 egg whites
1 tbsp superfine sugar	

Cut the melon into large wedges and scoop the flesh and juices into a large freezer container. Reserve a few of the seeds. Stir the sugar into the watermelon liquid and freeze for 3–4 hours until firm around the edges and slushy in the center. Beat thoroughly (this is most easily done in a food processor). With clean beaters, beat the egg whites in a large bowl until they form soft peaks. Fold into the ice mixture with the reserved seeds, if wished. Return to the freezer and freeze for 4–6 hours or until firm.

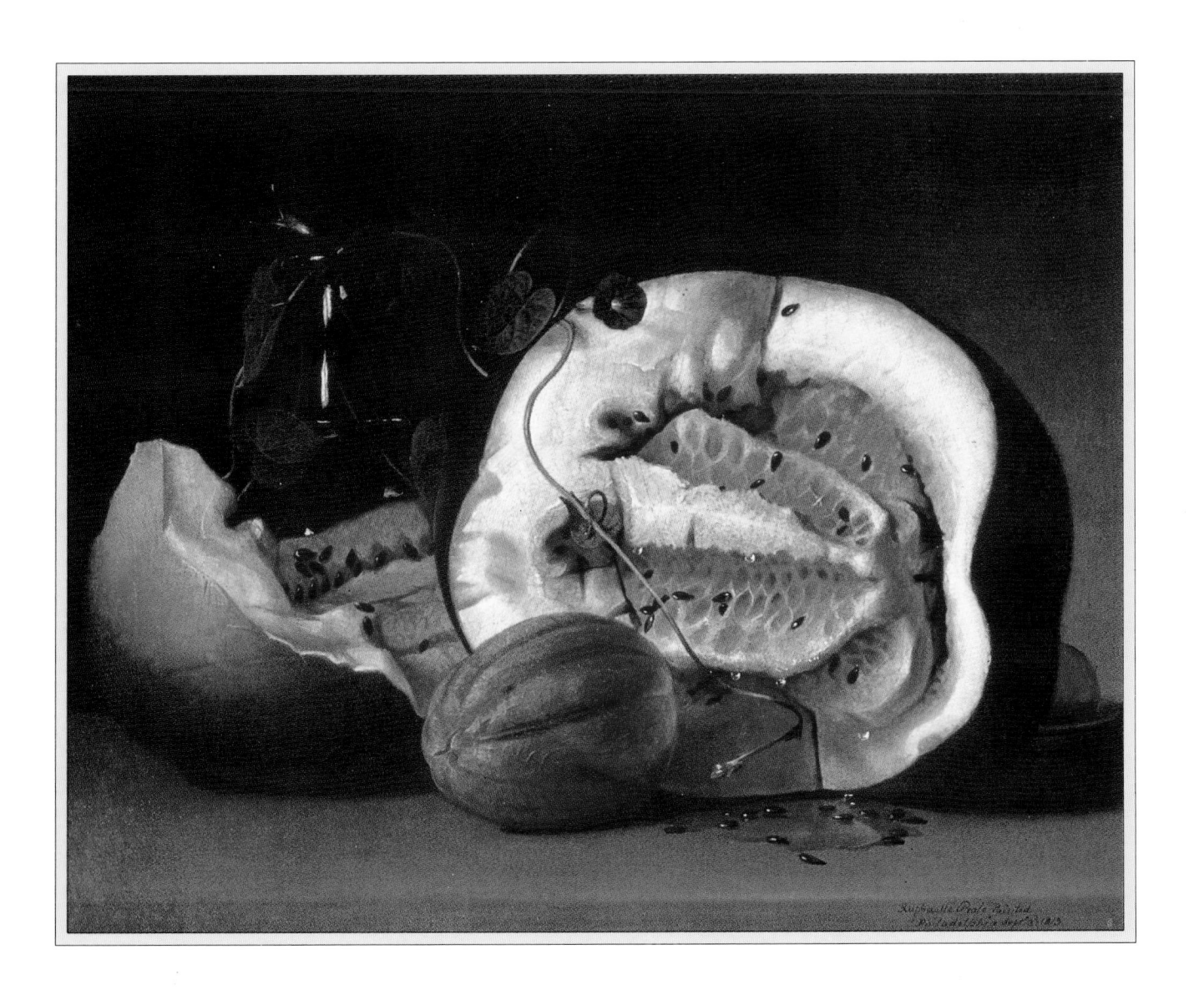

THE OPEN-AIR BREAKFAST

William Merritt Chase (1849–1916)

OHIO (TOLEDO MUSEUM OF ART)

William Merritt Chase was one of the foremost exponents of the American Impressionist school. He was very prolific and produced in his long life genre scenes of the American upper classes, such as the delightful example here, landscapes and still lifes. Although his roots as a painter were in the European tradition, his subjects have a strong American flavor. But the flavor of America was not always to the taste of European visitors, as Charles Dickens has related.

Dickens went to America for the first time in 1842 (when he was 30). In the published account of his travels, *American Notes*, he was often critical and the Americans were not best pleased. Late in his life he toured America again, giving hugely successful readings from his works. His lugubrious rendition of "The Death of Little Nell" was enormously popular and all over the country had audiences in packed theaters sobbing.

Traveling on a canal boat in Pennsylvania during the first journey Dickens recounted, "The next morning at 8 o'clock breakfast everybody sat down to the tea, coffee, butter, salmon, shad, liver, steak, potatoes, pickles, ham-chops, black puddings, and sausages all over again . . . Dinner was breakfast again without the tea and coffee; and supper and breakfast were identical." On another occasion he wrote, "Breakfast would have been no breakfast unless the principal dish were a deformed beefsteak with a great flat bone in the center, swimming in hot butter and sprinkled with the very blackest of all possible pepper."

Meat is still prominent on the American breakfast table but generally in the form of bacon or sausages. What the eyes of the world perceive as typically American, however, is the enormous variety of American breakfast breads and hot cakes. As the culinary historian Richard J. Hooker writes in *Food and Drink in America*, "The varieties of hot cakes were legion and had such names as rice cakes, corn cakes, griddle cakes, flannel cakes, buttermilk cakes, sour-milk cakes, flap jacks, slap jacks, hominy cakes, buckwheat cakes and various waffles and fritters." But the same author states that from the late 18th century the upper and middle classes served fruit at breakfast and quotes the Virginian cookery writer Mary Terhume in 1875 remarking that "the presence of the fruit basket at the breakfast table had recently become so common that its absence, when fruits were ripe, would be noticed and even 'felt painfully' by some . . ."

The elegant family in this sunny painting would certainly have had fruit for breakfast but the popovers below from the *Boston Cook Book* by Mary Lincoln, published in 1883, would not have been out of place.

BREAKFAST POPOVERS

"One cup flour, 1 saltspoonful salt, 1 cup milk, 1 egg yolk and white beaten separately. Mix the salt with the flour; add part of the milk slowly, until a smooth paste is formed; add the remainder of the milk with the beaten yolk, and lastly the white beaten to a stiff froth. Cook in hot buttered gem pans or earthen cups in a quick oven for half-an-hour, or until the puffs are brown and well popped over."

Makes about 12

1 cup all-purpose flour, sifted	1 egg, yolk and white
½tsp salt	beaten separately
1 cup milk	

Follow the original recipe, but use buttered muffin tins. Bake in a pre-heated oven, 425°F, for 20–30 minutes.

IN THE STUDIO

Octave Tassaert (1800–74)

PARIS (LOUVRE)

This portrait of a pale, handsome young artist in his studio is typical of the 19th-century romantic view of bohemian life. It is an idealized picture of poverty. His lodgings are humble but not squalid. He is eating potatoes – the food of the poor – but the scene is still a cheerful one with a cosy fire and a well-fed cat. The grim reality was the Irish potato famine which was raging at the time this picture was painted and the Irish peasantry who were starving to death.

Discovered by the Spanish in the Andes mountains in 1534, the potato was brought back to Spain within the next few years and enjoyed at first a spectacular reputation as a medicine, in particular as a cure for impotence. By the end of the 16th century, it was eaten in both Spain and Italy, soon spreading to the Lowlands (or Netherlands).

In England, where it was introduced by either Sir John Hawkins, Sir Francis Drake or Sir Walter Raleigh (there is much debate on this issue) in the last half of the 16th century, the potato had a brief vogue as an expensive curiosity.

The only nation to adopt the potato with whole-hearted enthusiasm was the Irish, who by the 17th century consumed it to the exclusion of almost every other food. This exclusivity was to prove a disaster for the Irish during the potato famines of the later 1840s.

The French, the last Europeans to accept the potato, regarded it with the deepest suspicion. In 1749 one French agricultural expert called it the worst of all vegetables. In Burgundy, cultivation was forbidden by law, and in 1771 the French Government directed the medical faculty in Paris to determine whether or not the potato was safe to eat.

The primary promoter of the potato in France was the apothecary to the Army, Parmentier, who had survived a year as a prisoner of war in Prussia during the Seven Years' War (1756–63) on a diet mainly of potatoes. His first attempts at proselytizing were greeted with powerful resistance. He was sacked from his job after the pensioners at the Hôtel des Invalides complained of being fed "pig fodder." In 1769 he entered the potato in a competition held by the city of Besançon to find the best plant that could be used as a substitute for grain cereals in case of famine, and won first prize. He gave a dinner party – Benjamin Franklin was among the guests – at which potatoes were cooked in 20 different ways. But his greatest triumph came on August 25, 1775, when he presented Louis XVI and Marie Antoinette with bouquets of potato flowers and was gratified to hear the King proclaim that the potato meant an end to famine.

It was not, however, until the desperate times during the French Revolution and the famine of 1816 that the potato was finally universally accepted.

The recipe below for Potatoes à la Provençal comes from Alan and Jane Davidson's translation of an edited version of Alexandre Dumas père's *Grand Dictionnaire de Cuisine* (published as *Dumas on Food*). Dumas (1802–70), apart from writing scores of plays and novels, was also a considerable gourmet and an accomplished cook.

POMMES DE TERRE A LA PROVENCAL

"Put six soupspoons of oil in a casserole with the zest of the lemon, parsley, garlic, and well-chopped spring onion, a little grated nutmeg, salt and pepper. Then peel the potatoes, and cook them with these seasonings. When the moment to serve arrives, sprinkle them with the juice of a lemon."

PROVENÇAL POTATOES

Serves 8

6tbsp oil	2 scallions, finely
Grated rind and juice of	chopped
½ lemon	Grated nutmeg
2tbsp chopped fresh	Salt and pepper
parsley	1½lb potatoes,
1 garlic clove, crushed	cut into chunks

Follow the original recipe but cover the pan tightly and cook over a low heat for 15–20 minutes until tender, shaking the pan occasionally.

BOSTON BAKED BEANS

Anon, American, 19th century

NEW YORK (NEW YORK HISTORICAL SOCIETY)

The baked bean is an icon of American culture, second only to Coca-Cola. The late Waverley Root in his encyclopedia, *Food*, credits the American Indians with its invention. But other Indian food listed by Mr. Root would not be out of place on the menu of any smart "ethnic" restaurant today. The Seminoles in Florida cooked fish with wild grapes, the Iroquois stuffed duck with them. In New England, huckleberries and blackberries were added to stews, the wild beach plums were made into jam, and buffalo berries were used for a sauce for buffalo meat. The Hopi put deep-fried squash blossoms into meat dishes, while the north-western tribes flavored roast meat, stews and salmon with juniper berries.

Pit cooking, taught by the American Indians to the earliest settlers, which was used before pots were made, remained in favor, Root writes, because of the superior flavor long, even, slow cooking gives. The pit method of cooking became the "bean-hole" used in the vast lumber camps of Maine and the upper Mississippi; baked beans were the most important food of the lumber jacks.

New Englanders perfected the art of the boiled one-pot dinner. The severe climate meant that fires were needed for almost nine months of the year and provided heat all day long, over which the great iron pots could simmer. The Indians were said to have flavored their pit-cooked beans with maple sugar and a lump of bear fat. New Englanders used butter, maple sugar, pork, and molasses.

The original version may have been sweetened but at least one 19th-century cookery writer, Mary Cornelius, in *The Young Housekeeper's Friend*, stated, as though it were something new, that "many persons think it a decided improvement to put in a large spoonful or 2 of molasses. It is a very good way."

The version given by Lydia Maria Child in *The American Frugal Housewife – Dedicated to Those who are not ashamed of Economy*, published in Boston in 1832, may be regarded as a definitive early one and probably accounts for the name by which baked beans are known in America – Boston Baked Beans. The recipe is given below.

There is hardly another canned food that has gained the universal acceptance of the baked bean. The first cannery in America to market pork and beans was in Portland, Maine, in 1875. In 1891 the Van Camp company in Indianapolis added the tomatoes to the recipe, a formula still used today.

BOSTON BAKED BEANS

"Baked beans are a very simple dish, yet few cook them well. They should be put in cold water and hung over the fire the night before they are baked. In the morning, they should be put in a colander, and rinsed 2 or 3 times; then again placed in a kettle with the pork you intend to bake, covered with water, and kept scalding hot, an hour or more. A pound of pork is quite enough for a quart of beans, and that is a large dinner for a common family. The rind of the pork should be slashed. Pieces of pork, alternately fat and lean, are the most suitable; the cheeks are the best. A little pepper sprinkled among the beans, when they are placed in the bean-pot will render them less unhealthy. They should be covered with water when put into the oven; and the pork should be sunk a little below the surface of the beans. Bake 3 or 4 hours."

Serves 8

1½lb Boston beans	Salt and pepper
(Haricot beans)	3tbsp soft brown sugar
1lb streaky belly pork	1tbsp wholegrain mustard

Put the beans in a large bowl and cover with boiling water. Leave to soak overnight.

Drain the beans and put them in a large saucepan, cover them with fresh water and bring to the boil. Boil vigorously for 10 minutes, drain and rinse. Cut the pork into 'bite-sized' pieces. Layer the beans and pork in a large casserole dish, seasoning lightly with salt and pepper. Combine the sugar and mustard with 1½pt boiling water and pour over the layered beans and pork. Cover with a tightly fitting lid and bake at 350°F for 2–2½ hours until the beans and pork are tender.

Bazaar Scene with Spices, *Anon, Indian, c. 1840*
Victoria & Albert Museum, London.

CHAPTER SIX

EASTERN
DELIGHTS

Unusual dishes and foods from the

Far East

EUROPEAN LADIES EATING BY A RIVER

Indian, 17th century

LONDON (BRITISH LIBRARY)

The European ladies enjoying their sweetmeats by the river probably did not, in reality, pop quite so alarmingly out of their dresses as they do in this painting by an Indian artist.

The dainty sweets these finely, if immodestly, dressed ladies of leisure are eating were introduced to India by the great Moguls, who established their imperial power in India in the 16th century. The courtly Mughlai cooking of Muslim Isfahan in Persia with its kebabs, pilau rice dishes with shredded meat, fruit and nuts; almonds, almond milk and rosewater, and its splendid practice of decorating food with edible gold and silver tissue, was absorbed into Indian cuisine. Candy, which comes from the Arabic word for sugar, was adopted in the sub-continent with relish. Mixtures of sugar and almonds, sugar and rice flour and sugar and coconut, as well as plain sugar candies, became popular all over India.

Perhaps the resident Hindus took to sweets with such enthusiasm because their ancient Sanskrit texts of Ayurvedic learning said that "a taste that is pleasant, proves comfortable to man, and contributes toward his life preservation; that keeps his mouth moist and increases the amount of bodily phlegm is called sweet . . . In Benares they say, 'A life is well lost that is lost in gorging sweets'."

Indian sweets, however, were not what fashionable Europe craved. After the East India Companies were formed in the early 1600s exotic food and furnishings from India were in huge demand. Europeans began to copy the expensive imported chintz fabrics and home cooks attempted to recreate the catsups and pickles of the East.

Pickled herbs, vegetables, mushrooms and flowers had been used extensively to garnish meat and fish dishes, stews, hashes and winter salads in the 16th century in Britain, but the jars of pickled mangoes brought back by the traders started a fad for versions made with the more easily obtainable cucumbers, onions or peaches.

An English recipe of 1694 "To pickle Lila, an Indian Pickle" consisted of cabbage, cauliflower, celery and other vegetables in a brine of vinegar with ginger, garlic, pepper, mustard seed and turmeric.

Oriental sauces were also copied. Catsups of mushrooms, anchovy and walnuts and the spicy fruit mangoes and chutneys were the originals of the modern sauces and chutneys that are still a British addiction. By the 1780s that stand-by of the modern spice shelf, pre-mixed curry powder, appeared in English cookbooks.

This recipe for a Mysore Pineapple Chutney comes from *Indian Pickles and Chutneys* by Aroona Roejhsinghani, Orient Paperbacks, Delhi, 1977. This is a modern Indian cookbook but as Indian cooking is traditional the recipe would presumably have been familiar to the ladies in the painting.

MYSORE PINEAPPLE CHUTNEY

"One pineapple, 2 green chilies, minced, 1 small onion, minced, ¼ teaspoon mustard seeds, ½ cup sugar, ½ teaspoon each of salt and powdered cumin seeds, and a few sliced mint and coriander leaves. Core and dice pineapple finely. Heat 2 tablespoons oil, add mustard seeds and when they stop popping, add onion and chillies and cook till soft. Add the remaining ingredients. Mix well, and remove from the fire. Serve after 1 hour."

Makes 2 jars

2tbsp oil	Heaped ½ cup sugar
¼tsp mustard seeds	½tsp salt
1 small onion, minced	½tsp ground cumin
1-2 green chilies, minced, deseeded	A few mint and coriander leaves, chopped
1lb fresh pineapple, peeled and cubed	

Heat the oil, add the mustard seeds and when they are popping, add the onion and chillies; cook them gently until tender. Add the remaining ingredients. Mix well, stir to dissolve the sugar, remove from the heat and cool. More like a relish, this should be eaten within two days.

THE COLLATION

Beauvais Tapestry, c. 1690–1745

MALIBU (THE J. PAUL GETTY MUSEUM)

The series of tapestries known as "The Story of the Emperor of China" were woven at the Beauvais factory in France around 1690 to 1705. The arms of the Comte de Toulouse, Louis-Alexandre de Bourbon (1678–1737), are woven into the border. He was an illegitimate son of King Louis XIV and Madame de Montespan and became an Admiral when he was only three years old.

The 1718 inventory of the count's château at Rambouillet listed six of the tapestries in the *antichambre du roi*, three in the *chambre du roi* and one in a storeroom above the stables. King Louis-Philippe (1773–1880) inherited eight of them and they were among his effects sold in 1852. Of the ten in the set, two, *The Audience of the Emperor* and *The Emperor on a Journey*, were owned by the Empress Eugénie (1826–1920), who hung them in the Château of Compiègne, where they are today.

The Chinese Emperor so lavishly depicted in his exotic surroundings was probably K'ang-hsi (1661–1721), the second emperor of the Ching dynasty, which lasted from 1644 until 1911, when Sun Yat-sen became President of the Chinese republic.

One of his most important achievements was opening four ports to foreign trade which lifted the veils that had shrouded China in mystery for centuries. He also encouraged the introduction of Western education, art and religion. Known all his life as an enthusiastic scholar, K'ang-hsi employed several Jesuit missionaries and was taught geometry by Ferdinand Verbiest, who later became Deputy Director of the Imperial Observatory. Scientists, including Jean-Baptiste Regis and Pierre Jartoux, were commissioned to compile an accurate atlas of the Empire.

The opening of China to foreigners, together with works such as the *Atlas* and the vast imports into the west of Chinese porcelain and lacquer by the East India Companies in the early decades of the 17th century, stimulated the interest of Europeans. Most of the royals of Europe were avid collectors, eager to adorn their palaces with the new and wonderful Chinese imports.

This savory dish comes from *The Court and Country Cook*, an English translation, published in 1691, of *Le cuisinier Royal et Bourgeois*, by an author known as Massialot, who worked for the Dukes of Chartres and Orléans.

CASSEROLE WITH RICE

"Boil your rice in a pot and make a ragoo with morilles, common mushrooms, truffles, veal sweetbreads, cock's combs and artichoke bottoms. If you please, add the combs and morilles may be farc'd and dress'd apart and afterwards put into the ragoo. Then make an essence with 2 or 3 cloves of garlic, sweet basil, cloves and wine and let all boil together, strain the liquor through a sieve and pour it into the ragoo. If you have a large fat pullet or any other tame or wild fowl, to be served up with your soup, lay it in a convenient dish, put the ragoo to it and cover neatly with rice, leaving a little fat on the top to render it smooth and cause it to come to a color in the oven. If there be no fowl at hand but only a good loin of mutton boiled, put it in like manner into a dish, when it is well dress'd and cover it very thick with rice. Then spread on top some fat with bacon to give it a colour."

Serves 4

3tbsp oil	2 cloves garlic, crushed
4 chicken portions	2tbsp fresh basil, chopped
1 large onion, chopped	2 cloves
8oz long grain rice	½pt dry white wine
6oz veal sweetbreads, cut into ½in pieces	½pt chicken stock
	Salt and pepper
4oz mushrooms, quartered	
A 14oz can artichoke hearts, drained	

Heat the oil in a pan and brown the chicken portions. Drain and place in the bottom of a large casserole dish. Fry the onion and rice for 5 minutes, add the sweetbreads to brown. Add to the chicken, with the rest of the ingredients. Cover and cook at 400°F for 1½ hours or until rice and chicken are tender. Season to taste and serve.

HARVESTING PINEAPPLES

Beauvais Tapestry, c. 1690–1705

MALIBU (THE J. PAUL GETTY MUSEUM)

The pineapples being so daintily and unrealistically harvested in this tapestry would have been rare and strange to the Comte de Toulouse, for whom the elaborate hanging was made. The flavor and fragrance of the pineapple had "astonished and delighted" Christopher Columbus and his men when they tasted it in Guadeloupe on their second voyage to the West Indies. The first accurate description of it by a European was written in 1535 by Oviedo Valdes, who said its delicious taste combined the flavors of melons, strawberries, raspberries and pippins (apples), and that although it grew on a plant like a thistle, it was "in taste, one of the best fruits in the world."

The Comte de Toulouse's father, King Louis XIV, was presented with the first pineapple grown in France. The King, who was known for being greedy, bit into the unfamiliar fruit before it was peeled and cut his lip badly on the sharp spines. As a result, they did not find royal favor until his successor, Louis XV, constructed a special greenhouse for them.

At much the same period, the English monarch, Charles I, was also enjoying pineapples. John Evelyn wrote in his diary (which began in 1640) that "standing by his Majesty at dinner in the presence, there was of that rare fruit called the King-pine, growing in Barbadoes and the East Indies, the first of these that ever I had seen. His Majesty, having cut it up, was pleased to give me a piece off his own plate to taste of; but, in my opinion, it falls short of those ravishing varieties of deliciousness described in Captain Ligon's History, and others, but possibly, it might be, or certainly was, much impaired in coming so far; it has yet a graceful acidity, but tastes more like the quince and melon than of any other."

Pineapples were rare in the 18th century and a search of cookbooks of that time has not revealed any recipes for them. Louis Eustache Ude was one of the many French chefs who worked in England. He was employed by the Earl of Sefton and later at Crockford's Gaming Club. His book *The French Chef* was published in London in 1813.

PINE-APPLE JELLY

"The pine-apple, although a very odoriferous fruit, is not very juicy. Clarify some sugar, take the rind of a pine-apple, and turn the best part equally. Let it be of the diameter of a crown-piece, but a little thicker. Boil it in the sugar, squeeze into the syrup the juice of a lemon or two, and put to it some isinglass ready clarified. Strain the whole through a bag, drain the pine-apples through a clean hair sieve; next put in the mould a little of the pine-apple jelly; and when these are about three-eighths of an inch deep at the bottom of the mould, put the mould on ice to freeze. When firm lay slices of pine-apple symmetrically over the jelly. Mind that they are quite dry, and use a little jelly to make them stick together. When the jelly is frozen to a substance, put in a little more to freeze again; then fill the mould, and put some ice all round. If the pine-apple does not look well enough to be served in the jelly, send up the jelly by itself, but keep the slices of the fruit in sugar, as they will serve another day to make pine-apple fritters."

Serves 4

1 fresh pineapple	Juice of 1 lemon
2½ cups water	1 tbsp powdered gelatin
Heaped ½ cup sugar	

Slice the pineapple and cut away the skin. Remove the hard core and chop the fruit into chunks. Put the water and sugar into a saucepan and slowly bring to a boil, stirring occasionally to dissolve the sugar. Add the pineapple, cook for 15 minutes, then drain. Strain the juice through a fine strainer and reserve the pineapple pieces.

Put the lemon juice in a small bowl and sprinkle the gelatin over the top. Leave to soak and swell for a minute or two, then stir into the hot syrup until dissolved. Leave to cool until just beginning to set, stirring occasionally. Pour a little of the jelly into a wet mold or bowl. Add a few pieces of the pineapple and leave to set in a cool place. (Keep the rest of the jelly in a warm place to prevent it setting.)

Continue adding layers of jelly and fruit, letting each layer set before adding another. Leave to set completely, then dip the mold or bowl into hot water for a few seconds and turn out on to a serving plate.

LADIES AND BOYS IN A GARDEN

Persian, 19th century

LONDON (VICTORIA & ALBERT MUSEUM)

This painting of Persian Ladies and Boys is still cataloged in the Victoria and Albert Museum as "Anon," but B. W. Robinson, a former keeper in the Far Eastern Department, suggests that it is one of the three paintings known in Europe by Tsma'il Jala'ir, who was the most celebrated of the early pupils of the Dar al-Din-Funun (College of Art) in Persia (now Iran). The college was founded by Nasr al-Din Shah, who was a respected painter himself, to instruct Persian painters in the European style of painting known as Qajar, after the dynasty of that name which ruled Persia (Iran) from 1779–1925. The Qajars were a tribe of Turkish origin who had served the Safavid monarchs and seized power after the fall of the last Safavid, Karim Khan Zand. Under the rule of the second Qajar monarch, Fath'Ali Shah, contacts between Persia and the West were closer than they had ever been previously.

Persian painting had been influenced by Europe during the reign of Karim Khan Zand (1752–1779) in Shiraz but it was under Fath'Ali Shah (1798–1834) that the European style, combined with elements that were essentially Persian, became established as the official national style. Fath'Ali Shah was an impressive figure with flashing black eyes and a flowing beard of which, it was said, he was as proud as he was of his 159 sons. He commissioned countless portraits of himself, his family, ladies of the court, ministers, acrobats and exotic dancers. These pictures are extremely decorative and are powerful, if slightly naive, images.

Nasr al-Din Shah, who became king in the 1840s, made his first tour of Europe in 1873. When he returned to Persia he stripped the native school paintings from the walls of his palaces and replaced them with the treasures he had collected.

Qajar paintings went completely out of fashion and a large number of them were astutely collected before the first world war by the Amery brothers, Harold and Leopold, as Robinson writes, in bazaars and curio shops from Alexandria to Calcutta. After the Second World War, as part of a general resurgence and reappraisal of Victorian arts in general, Qajar paintings made a spectacular comeback with soaring prices. Paintings from the Amery collection bought by the Empress Farah of Iran were eventually hung in the Negarestan Museum in Teheran.

One of the ladies in this painting has in front of her a samovar, dishes of figs, pomegranates and a bowl of what appears to be *Rahat Lokum* or Turkish delight. The links with Turkey are strong. In classical times the Persian empire stretched from India to the Mediterranean and as the Qajars were Turkish before they were Persian it is not inappropriate to use a recipe from the *Turkish Cookery Book* compiled in 1862 by Turabi Effendi, now known to have been a translation of what is called the first Turkish cookbook.

In the chapter on "Sherbets, or Thin Syrups with Fruit in them" is this recipe for *Injir Khòshabi*.

INJIR KHÒSHABI

"Cut off the stalks of one or two pounds of figs, prick each one here and there with a wooden needle, place them in a basin with two or three pints of hot or cold water, and let them remain for ten or twelve hours; then pass the liquid through a sieve into a glass bowl, and add the figs with a few drops of orange-flower, and a few pieces of ice, and serve."

FIG SYRUP

Makes about 5 cups

1lb fresh figs	Few drops of orange
3¾ cups water	flower water
	Ice

Trim the stalks from the figs and prick them with a fork. Put in a large bowl with the water. Leave to soak for 10–12 hours or overnight. Drain the liquid through a strainer into a large pitcher. Stir in the figs, the orange flower water to taste and the ice. Serve at once.

STILL LIFE WITH MANGOES

Paul Gauguin (1848–1903)

(PRIVATE COLLECTION)

Paul Gauguin painted these luscious mangoes around 1896, not long after he had returned to the South Sea Islands for the last time.

Although he was born in Paris (in 1848), his mother's family came from Peru and he spent part of his childhood there. He was a stockbroker in Paris in 1872, and also an amateur painter, who both collected the works of the Impressionists and exhibited with them from 1880–86. In 1883 he gave up his job to live and paint in Brittany. In 1887, he visited Panama and Martinique and in 1888 he spent two traumatic months with Vincent van Gogh in Arles. He went to Tahiti in 1891, but when he ran out of money in 1893 he returned to Paris. He was seriously injured in a brawl with sailors in Brittany in 1894 and, in spite of ill-health, returned to the South Pacific in 1895. His last years – he died at Atuana in the Marquesas in 1903 – were overshadowed by poverty and illness.

Mangoes are the fruit of a tropical evergreen tree, *Mangifera indica*, a relative of both the cashew and the pistachio. It is a native of India, which is still the world's greatest producer of mangoes. Alexander the Great's men saw mango trees growing in the Indus valley in 327 BC. In 1673 a traveler discussing the taste of the mango said that the "Nectarine, Peach and Apricot fall short," and another reported in 1727 that "the Goa mango is reckoned the largest and most delicious to the taste of any in the world and, I may add, the wholesomest and best tasted of any fruit in the world." Many Indians say the small, exquisitely scented, sweet Alfonso mango is the best.

Mangoes are said to have been planted in Africa by Persian traders around AD 1000 and by 1700 they were planted in Brazil. By 1740 they had reached the West Indies and tropical Australasia. Mangoes were growing in southern Florida, the only state in which they flourish, and were first grown in 1825, but they became a commercial success only after 1889, when the United States Department of Agriculture improved the grafted varieties. The original Indian mango, *mulgoba*, has an excellent flavor but only a moderate yield. The "Hayden" is the variety mainly grown and exported now.

There were few recipes for mangoes, except for pickles, other than in Indian cooking, at the time Gauguin lived. Therefore I make no apology for including a recipe that my mother made up. When I was nine, my parents bought a fruit grove in southern Florida where 40 acres of avocado, papaya, lime and mango groves provided them with a constant supply of fresh sub-tropical produce. Being a perverse child I hankered after the cherries, apples and pears of my early childhood and did not really appreciate mango pie until I made it myself.

EDNA-MAY'S MANGO PIE

"Shortcrust pastry for a 2-crust pie, 2 large ripe mangos, peeled and sliced, sprinkling of sugar, freshly grated nutmeg.

Line a pie dish with half of the pastry, arrange the mango slices on top of it, sprinkle with sugar and nutmeg, cover with the rest of the pastry, pinch the edges, slash with a knife in a few places and bake in a moderately hot oven until the pastry is browned. You may sprinkle sugar (before cooking) on top of the pie if you wish."

Serves 6

½lb piecrust dough	Freshly grated nutmeg
2 large ripe mangos, peeled, stoned and sliced	1 egg, beaten
2tbsp soft light brown sugar	1tbsp unrefined brown sugar

Roll out two-thirds of the dough on a floured surface and use to line an 8-in pie plate. Fill the dough-lined plate with the mangos and sprinkle with the soft brown sugar and nutmeg to taste. Roll out the remaining dough for a lid. Damp the edge of the pie and cover with the dough, pressing the edges together to seal. Brush the top of the pie with beaten egg and sprinkle with the sugar. Bake in a preheated oven, 400°F, for 30 minutes.

THREE GIRLS

Koriusa, 19th century

The delicate ladies in this woodcut are typical of the art form instantly recognizable as Japanese to the Western eye. Japanese graphic artists perfected the technique of woodcut printing which strongly influenced Western artists at the end of the last century. The many European artists who incorporated Japanese elements into their work include Van Gogh, Whistler and Edvard Munch.

Japanese food, however, was almost unknown outside the Orient until the last few decades. Perhaps this is because few Japanese opened restaurants abroad or because the severe purity of Japanese cuisine is more difficult to achieve (or assimilate) than, say, the more robust food of China.

The eminent exponent of Japanese cuisine, Shizuo Tsuji, who runs a professional culinary institute in Osaka, explains the principles of Japanese cooking in the elegant preface to his *magnum opus, Japanese Cooking – A Simple Art* (1980).

The essence of Japan's culture and its cooking is their closeness to nature. As in Japanese painting and poetry the cuisine is "simply the result of an acute awareness of the seasons." This is also a culture born of austerity; even in the Imperial court of ancient Kyoto – "impoverished but cultivated" – a cuisine was developed to utilize each season's offerings with the utmost artistry. Each of the many small courses that make up a Japanese meal is a separate work of art.

The key ingredients, he explains, are a "rather delicate" stock, *dashi*, made from *konbu* (giant kelp) and flakes of dried bonito fish and *shoyu* (Japanese soy sauce). The other essentials for successful Japanese cooking are ingredients in prime condition and of pristine freshness and beautiful presentation.

Tsuji's first rule for the modern cook is to avoid frozen food. The Japanese have always used dried food, but freezing destroys texture. Freshness and naturalness are the key – the unnatural and artificial have no place in Japanese cuisine. "If you live inland or in the mountains, do not cook seafood. Eat river fish and those caught in local lakes and streams. And eat them straight away, while they are fresh."

One modern invention the master does commend is instant *dashi* – far superior to the stock cubes of the West, which he suggests "are terrible."

The simple soup is a basic element of a Japanese meal. As Tsuyi says, the combination of fresh seasonal ingredients and non-seasonal basic ingredients makes each miso soup different.

MISO-SHIRU

'**3** ½ cups dashi, ½ cup nameko mushrooms or 2 shitake mushrooms, soaked and sliced, ⅓ cake tofu (bean curd), 4tbsp redfmiso (aka miso, made from barley), 4 stalks trefoil (similar to parsley and available from Japanese soups), ground sansho pepper (a reddish-brown pepper, the pod of the prickly ash).

Drain the tofu. Soften the miso in a medium-sized bowl by adding 2tbsp tepid stock and blending with a wire whisk. If you put the miso soup directly into the stock pot, it will not be properly held in solution and the soup will be full of miso pellets. Gradually ladle the softened miso into the stock in a medium-sized pot, simmering over medium heat. When all the miso has been added and is dissolved, add the solid ingredients. The tofu can be cut into ½in cubes over the stock pot. Chop the trefoil stalks into small pieces. Keep soup at a simmer a few minutes until mushrooms and tofu are heated. Remove from heat just before boiling point. Ladel into individual lacquer bowls distributing the mushrooms, tofu and chopped trefoil equally and attractively. Garnish with a shake or two of sansho pepper. Cover and serve immediately.'

MISO SOUP

Serves 6–8

¼lb tofu	2 shiitake mushrooms,
4tbsp red miso	soaked and thinly sliced
3¾ cups clear stock	4 stalks trefoil, chopped
2 sachets dushi	Pinch ground sansho pepper

Follow the original method.

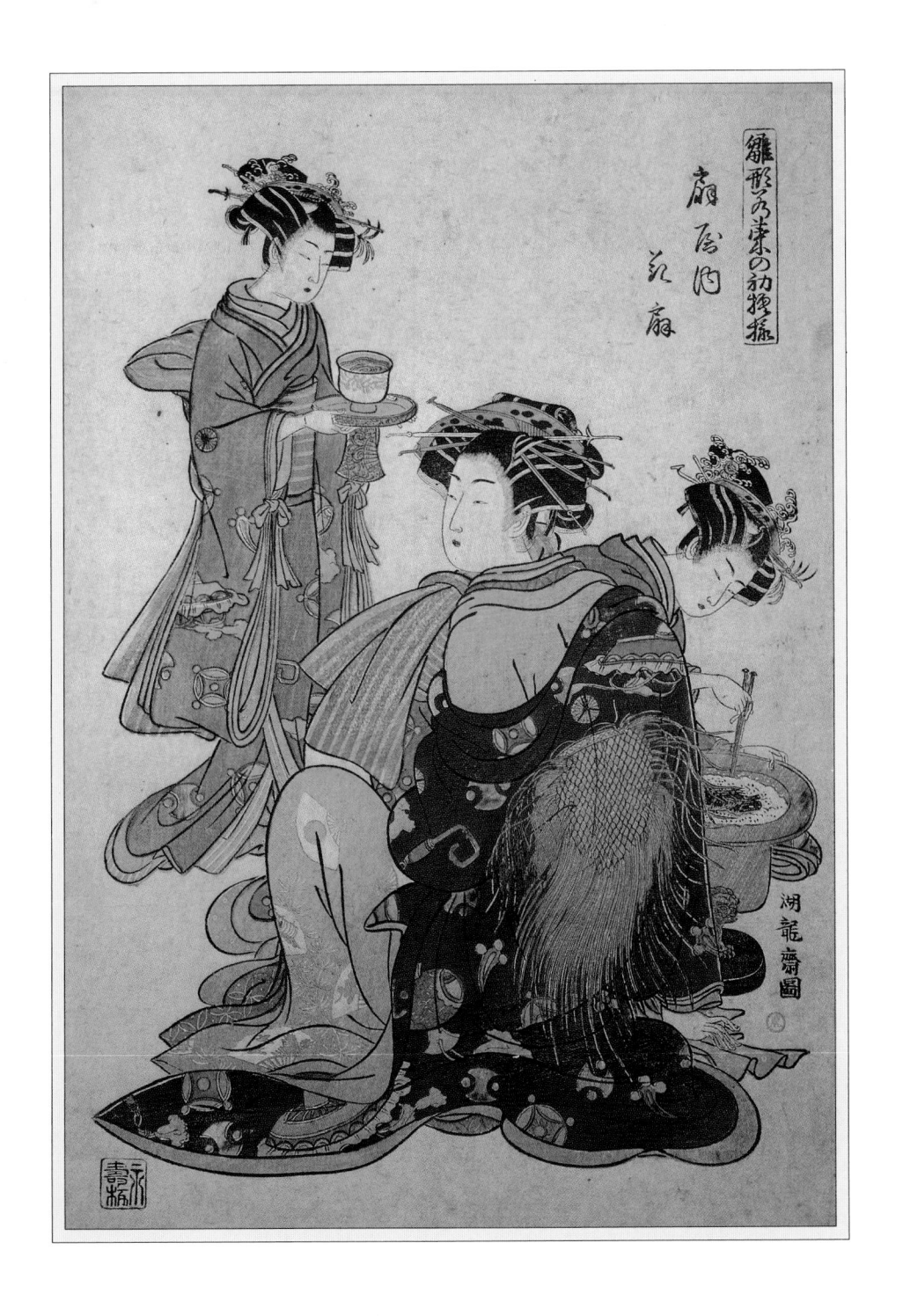

MENU FOR AN ITALIAN BANQUET

FIRST COURSE

Cold Delicacies from the Sideboard

Pieces of marzipan and marzipan balls

Neapolitan spice cakes

Malaga wine and Pisan biscuits

Plain pastries made with milk and eggs

Fresh grapes

Spanish olives

Prosciutto cooked in wine, sliced, and served with capers, grape pulp, and sugar

Salted pork tongues cooked in wine, sliced

Spit-roasted songbirds, cold, with their tongues sliced over them

Sweet mustard

SECOND COURSE

Hot Foods from the Kitchen: Roasts

Fried veal sweetbreads and liver, with a sauce of eggplant, salt, sugar, and pepper

Spit-roasted skylarks with lemon sauce

Spit-roasted quails with sliced aubergines

Stuffed spit-roasted pigeons with sugar and capers sprinkled over them

Spit-roasted rabbits, with sauce and crushed pine nuts

Partridges, larded and spit-roasted, served with lemon slices

Pastries filled with minced veal sweetbreads and served with slices of prosciutto

Strongly seasoned poultry with lemon slices and sugar

Slices of veal, spit-roasted, with a sauce made from the juices

Leg of goat, spit-roasted, with a sauce made from the juices

Soup of almond cream, with the flesh of three pigeons for every two guests

Squares of meat aspic

Bartolomeo Scappi reproduced the menu he arranged for his employer Pope Pius V in his Opera *published in 1570.*

THIRD COURSE

Hot Foods from the Kitchen: Boiled Meats and Stews

Stuffed fat geese, boiled Lombard style and covered with sliced almonds, served with cheese, sugar, and cinnamon

Stuffed breast of veal, boiled, garnished with flowers

Milk calf, boiled, garnished with parsley

Almonds in garlic sauce

Turkish-style rice with milk, sprinkled with sugar and cinnamon

Stewed pigeons with mortadella sausage and whole onions

Cabbage soup with sausages

Poultry pie, two chickens to each pie

Fricasseed breast of goat dressed with fried onions

Pies filled with custard cream

Boiled calves' feet with cheese and egg

FOURTH COURSE

Delicacies from the Sideboard

Bean tarts

Quince pastries, one quince per pastry

Pear tarts, the pears wrapped in marzipan

Parmesan cheese and Riviera cheese

Fresh almonds on vine leaves

Chestnuts roasted over the coals and served with salt, sugar, and pepper

Milk curds with sugar sprinkled over

Ring-shaped cakes   Wafers

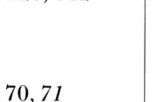

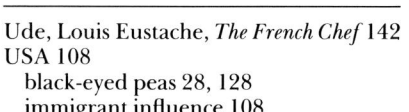
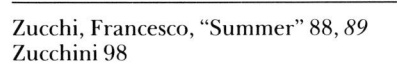

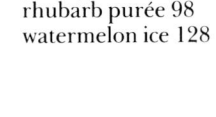

BIBLIOGRAPHY

ALPERS, SVETLANA
The Art of Describing: Dutch Art in the Seventeenth Century.
JOHN MURRAY, LONDON, 1983.

ARESTY, ESTHER B.
The Exquisite Table.
BOBBS-MERRILL, INDIANAPOLIS/NEW YORK, 1980.

BARBER, RICHARD
Cooking & Recipes from Rome to the Renaissance.
ALLEN LANE, LONDON, 1973

BAUMAN, JAMES. "LES GALETTES DES ROIS"
Petits Propos Culinaires 27 (1980).

CLAIR, COLIN
Kitchen and Table
ABELARD-SCHUMAN, LONDON, 1964

COE, SOPHIE. "AZTEC CUISINE"
Petits Propos Culinaires, Parts I, II, III; 19, 20, 21 (1985).

COYLE, PATRICK L.
The World Encyclopedia of Food
FACTS ON FILE, NEW YORK, 1982.

DARBY, WILLIAM J, GHALIOUNGUI, PAUL, GRIVETTI, LOUIS
Food: The Gift of Osiris
ACADEMIC PRESS, LONDON, NEW YORK, SAN FRANCISCO, 1977.

DAVIDSON, ALAN
Mediterranean Seafood (1972)
PENGUIN, LONDON, 1981.

DEL CONTE ANNA
Gastronomy of Italy
BANTAM PRESS, LONDON, 1987.

DE GRAMONT, SANCHE
Epitaph For Kings
DELTA, NEW YORK, 1967.

DE LA TOUR DU PIN, MADAME
Memoirs (edited and translated by Felice Harcourt)
CENTURY, LONDON, 1969.

DOUGLAS, MARY
Purity and Danger
ROUTLEDGE & KEGAN PAUL, LONDON, 1966.

ELIAS, NORBERT
The History of Manners (1939)
BASIL BLACKWELL, OXFORD, 1978.

GELB, BARBARA LEVINE (compiled by)
The Dictionary of Food
PADDINGTON PRESS, NEW YORK/LONDON, 1978.

GOODWIN, GILLIAN
Manchet & Trencher
GELOFER, LONDON, 1983.

GREER, GERMAINE
The Obstacle Race (1979)
PICADOR, LONDON, 1981.

GROUNDES-PEACE, ZARA (ed. Robin Howe)
Old Cookery Notebook
DAVID & CHARLES, LONDON, 1979.

HALL, JAMES
Subjects and Symbols in Art
JOHN MURRAY, LONDON, 1974.

HARRISON, S. G., MASEFIELD, G. B., AND WALLIS, MICHAEL
The Illustrated Book of Food Plants (published as *The Oxford Book of Food Plants,* 1969)
REPRINTED BY PEERAGE, LONDON, 1985.

HARTLEY, DOROTHY
Food in England
MACDONALD, LONDON, 1954.

HEDRICK, U. P. (ed.)
Sturtevant's Edible Plants of the World (1919)
DOVER, NEW YORK, 1972.

HENISCH, BRIDGET ANN
Cakes and Characters
PROSPECT BOOKS, LONDON, 1984.

HESS, JOHN L. AND KAREN
The Taste of America
GROSSMAN, NEW YORK, 1977.

HIBBERT, CHRISTOPHER
The Grand Tour
THAMES METHUEN, LONDON, 1987.

HICKMAN, PEGGY
A Jane Austen Household Book
DAVID & CHARLES, NEWTON ABBOT, 1977.

HIEATT, CONSTANCE B. AND SHARON BUTLER (eds.)
Curye On Inglysch
THE EARLY ENGLISH TEXT SOCIETY, OXFORD UNIVERSITY PRESS, LONDON, 1985.

HUXLEY, G.
Talking of Tea
THAMES AND HUDSON, LONDON, 1956.

HOOKER, RICHARD J.
A History of Food and Drink in America
BOBBS-MERRILL, INDIANAPOLIS/NEW YORK, 1981.

KLEIN, MAGGIE BLYTH
The Feast of the Olive
ARIS BOOKS, BERKELEY, 1983.

MENNELL, STEPHEN
All Manners of Food
BASIL BLACKWELL, OXFORD, 1985.

MURRAY, PETER AND LINDA
Dictionary of Art & Artists
PENGUIN, LONDON.

NORMAN, BARBARA
Tales of the Table
PRENTICE-HALL, ENGLEWOOD CLIFFS, 1972.

OLIVER, RAYMOND
The French At Table
WINE AND FOOD SOCIETY, MICHAEL JOSEPH, LONDON, 1967.

ORIGO, IRIS
The Merchant of Prato (1957)
PENGUIN, LONDON, 1963.

PALMER, ARNOLD
Movable Feasts
OXFORD UNIVERSITY PRESS, LONDON, 1952.

POWER, EILEEN (editor and translator)
The Goodman of Paris
GEORGE ROUTLEDGE & SONS, LONDON, 1928.

PULLAR, PHILLIPA
Consuming Passions (1970)
BOOK CLUB ASSOCIATES, LONDON, 1977.

ROOT, WAVERLEY
The Food of France
CASSELL, LONDON, 1958.
The Food of Italy
VINTAGE, NEW YORK, 1977.
AND RICHARD DE ROCHEMONT
Eating in America
ECCO PRESS, NEW YORK (1976), 1981.
Food
SIMON AND SCHUSTER, NEW YORK, 1980.

RAO, SHIVAJI AND SHALINI DEVI HOLKAR
Cooking of the Maharajas
VIKING, NEW YORK, 1975.

REVEL, JEAN-FRANÇOIS
Culture and Cuisine (1979)
DOUBLEDAY & CO., GARDEN CITY, NEW YORK, 1982.

RUBINSTEIN, HELGE
The Chocolate Book (1981)
PENGUIN, LONDON, 1982.

SALAMAN, REDCLIFFE N.
The History and Social Influence of the Potato
CAMBRIDGE UNIVERSITY PRESS, CAMBRIDGE, 1949.

STERLING, CHARLES
Still Life Painting
HARPER & ROW, NEW YORK, 1981.

STOBART, TOM
The Cook's Encyclopaedia
B. T. BATSFORD, LONDON, 1980.

TANNAHIL, REAY
Food in History
STEIN AND DAY, NEW YORK, 1973.

TSUJI, SHIZUI
Japanese Cooking: A Simple Art
KODENSHA INTERNATIONAL, TOKYO, NEW YORK, SAN FRANCISCO, 1980.

VENCE, CÉLINE AND ROBERT COURTINE
The Grand Masters of French Cuisine
G. P. PUTNAM, NEW YORK, 1978.

WHEATON, BARBARA KETCHAM
Savoring the Past
UNIVERSITY OF PENNSYLVANIA, 1983.

WILSON, C. ANNE
Food and Drink in Britain
CONSTABLE, LONDON, 1973.
The Book of Marmalade
CONSTABLE, LONDON, 1985.

WILSON, GILLIAN, SASSOON, ADRIAN, AND BREMER-DAVID, CHARISSA
Acquisitions Made by the Department of Decorative Arts in 1983
THE J. PAUL GETTY MUSEUM JOURNAL, VOLUME 12, 1984.

AUTHOR'S ACKNOWLEDGMENTS

It would have been quite impossible for me to have completed this book without the help of many learned friends and colleagues. I would like to acknowledge my profound debt to all of the people who lent me books, looked for pictures, translated recipes and gave me much needed moral support. I would like to thank Sue Brill, Janet Clarke, Alan Davidson, Bamber and Christina Gascoigne, Elena Graves, Germaine Greer, John and Sheila Hale, Cecily Langdale, Edward Lucie-Smith, Ellen Lyons, Mike and Tess McKirdy, Martina Nicolls, Jenny Shaw, Nicolas Van Glann, Gillian Wilson, Joop Witteveen and especially, Colin Spencer.

Photo credit: JEAN HARVEY

PUBLISHER'S ACKNOWLEDGMENTS

The publishers would like to thank the following for their help in producing this book: Linda Frazer, Sue Maggs, Joy Law, Susan George, and Jill Ford.

Every effort has been made to trace and acknowledge all copyright holders; Quarto would like to apologize if any omissions have been made.

PICTURE CREDITS

Introduction:
Jacques Linard: *Basket of Fruit*, 17th cent. (Paris, Musée du Louvre) Edimedia

Anon., Flemish: *Feast in the House of Levy*, 15th cent. (Melbourne, National Gallery of Victoria)

p.11: Giraudon, Paris
p.13: Visual Arts Library, London
p.15: Scala, Florence
p.17: Visual Arts Library, London
p.19: Vienna, Nationalbibliothek
p.21: Edimedia, Paris
p.23: Visual Arts Library, London
p.25: Giraudon, Paris
p.27: Sotheby's, London
p.29: Scala, Florence
p.31: Visual Arts Library, London
p.33: Hubert Josse, Paris
p.35: Matthiesen Fine Arts, London
p.37: Scala, Florence
p.39: Scala, Florence
p.41: Bridgeman Arts Library, London
p.43: Edimedia, Paris
p.45: Plymouth Art Gallery
p.47: Edimedia, Paris
p.49: Pym's Gallery, London
p.51: Visual Arts Library, London
p.53: Visual Arts Library, London
p.55: Artothek, Planegg/Munich
p.57: The Marquess of Bath, Longleat

p.59: Matthiesen Fine Arts, London
p.61: Visual Arts Library, London
p.63: Edimedia, Paris
p.65: Yale Center for British Art, New Haven
p.67: Giraudon, Paris
p.69: Edimedia, Paris
p.71: Visual Arts Library, London
p.73: E.T. Archives, London
p.75: Scala, Florence
p.77: Scala, Florence
p.79: Réunion des Musées Nationaux, Paris
p.81: Scala, Florence
p.83: Réunion des Musées Nationaux, Paris
p.85: Visual Arts Library, London
p.87: Visual Arts Library, London
p.89: Edimedia, Paris
p.91: National Gallery of Scotland, Edinburgh
p.93: Art Gallery of Ontario, Toronto
p.95: Hubert Josse, Paris
p.97: Visual Arts Library, London
p.99: Giraudon, Paris
p.101: Tate Gallery, London
p.103: Tate Gallery, London
p.105: Bridgeman Arts Library

p.107: Edimedia, Paris
p.109: San Francisco Museum of Art
p.111: Public Records Office, London
p.113: National Portrait Gallery, London
p.115: Visual Arts Library, London
p.117: National Museum, Mexico
p.119: Scala, Florence
p.121: National Gallery, London
p.123: North Carolina Museum of Art, Raleigh
p.125: Tony Morrison, South American Pictures
p.127: Hubert Josse, Paris
p.129: Edimedia, Paris
p.131: Museum of Art, Toledo
p.133: Réunion des Musées Nationaux, Paris
p.135: Historical Society, New York
p.137: Victoria & Albert Museum, London
p.139: Visual Arts Library, London
p.141: J. Paul Getty Museum, Malibu
p.143: J. Paul Getty Museum, Malibu
p.145: Victoria & Albert Museum, London
p.147: Visual Arts Library, London
p.149: Victoria & Albert Museum, London